HOW TO WIN AT GOLF

HOW TO WIN AT GOLF

BRIAN CRAFTER with Bill Pritchard

Photography by Roger Gould

VIKING

Author's Note

To all of you who love golf and play the game, I dedicate this book. I have written as I teach and I hope that, with a little patience, common sense and intelligent observation, you may learn more about yourself and about your game.

Brian Crafter

Viking
Penguin Books Australia Ltd
487 Maroondah Highway, PO Box 257
Ringwood, Victoria 3134, Australia
Penguin Books Ltd
Harmondsworth, Middlesex, England
Viking Penguin, A Division of Penguin Books USA Inc.
375 Hudson Street, New York, New York 10014, USA
Penguin Books Canada Limited
10 Alcorn Avenue, Toronto, Ontario, Canada M4V 3B2
Penguin Books (N.Z.) Ltd
182–190 Wairau Road, Auckland 10, New Zealand

First published as *Winning Golf*
by Currey O'Neil Ross Pty Ltd 1983
First published by Penguin Books Australia Ltd 1987
Paperback edition published 1989

10 9 8 7 6 5 4 3

Produced by Penguin Books Australia Ltd in association with the Australian Broadcasting Corporation

Cover designed by Ron Hampton
Text designed by Tom Kurema
Typeset by ProComp Productions Pty Ltd, South Australia
Printed and bound in Hong Kong through Bookbuilders Limited

National Library of Australia
Cataloguing-in-Publication data

Crafter, Brian.
How to win at golf.

Includes index.
ISBN 0 670 90194 6.

1.Golf. I. Pritchard, Bill. II. Gould, Roger. III. Title.

796.352'3

Contents

1 Golf's Challenges

There's a well-reported story dating back some years when Jack Nicklaus was at his absolute peak. That was at a time when he seemed to be all but unbeatable.

The story goes that Nicklaus and his then heir-apparent, Johnny Miller, were offered $1 million to compete against each other in a single game of eighteen holes of golf. A million dollars for an afternoon's work—roughly $55 555 for each hole. Both men turned down the proposition as 'not being in the interests of the game'.

Well, it did happen quite a while ago, as I said, and a lot of mud has dried out since. Today, of course, million-dollar events are almost commonplace. The first million-dollar prize-money event was played in Africa at a mini-Las Vegas called Sun City. Ironically, Johnny Miller was among the invited players.

Despite the proliferation of such super tournaments, however, I do not believe the game of golf has reached the stage of say, tennis, where the desire to take up the sport is very often accompanied by the urge to make a lot of money. Golf has its mystiques, and I like to think that it remains the truest of sports. No matter what happens, no one can really alter the fact that golf is just you, the ball and the course.

The rules haven't been changed much; they are imposed from without, and, probably more importantly, from within. Bob Shearer provided us with a good example of the kind of internal discipline golf involves when he took a self-administered two-stroke penalty for grounding his club in a sandtrap during an Australian Open.

I see a golf course, with its spaciousness and natural beauty, as the perfect setting for this kind of self-examination. The routine of trying to get the ball into a hole perhaps 400 metres away can tell you a lot about yourself. It can provide relief from the problems and tensions of modern living and yet induce the mental stimulation most of us need. How well you meet that test depends ultimately on no one but you.

Bob Shearer

I was lucky enough to discover these things early. And here I hope you will pardon me for a digression — it has a bearing on what comes later.

My brother Murray and I had an upbringing which could be called normal for small boys in the early 1940s in Adelaide. Dad was away with the Air Force and things were fairly tight, especially in the pocket-money department. Caddying at the nearby Kooyonga Club provided a way out and, in turn, produced the incentive to start thumping the ball ourselves. It was a natural progression for us, later, to take up as young assistant professionals, learning how to make and use all clubs, and building our careers as professionals.

In tournament play, as things turned out, Murray usually had the edge; eleven times he was South Australian PGA champion, six times State Open champion and twice winner of the *Advertiser* Open tournament. So, it's a matter of some pride that I also won the *'Tiser* title, beating Murray on the way to shooting 275, the lowest winning score in the history of that particular tournament.

Those mid-1960s are, to me, the golden years of golf in Australia, and I regard myself as lucky to have been part of them. In peak form during those years were Peter Thomson, Kel Nagle, Frank Phillips, Bruce Devlin, Bruce Crampton, Eric Cremin, Norman Von Nida, Ossie Pickworth and from overseas, Bob Charles, Jack Nicklaus, Arnold Palmer and Gary Player.

Playing with and against them taught me many lessons and helped to build the foundations for my main career as a golf teacher.

From all this experience I learned to actually welcome the day-to-day grind as an opportunity to observe, ponder and put into practice, better ways to encourage people to improve and enjoy their golf.

Until 1973 I used a standard textbook approach. I simply passed on how to make the classic style of swing. Then, in that year, Lee Trevino came to the Lakes in Sydney for the Chrysler Classic. To watch him in close-up was a revelation.

Lee is a supremely natural man and his golf game reflects that. There is little that is standard about it. His swing, for instance, is flat and inside-out. To compensate for this he aims a long way to the left of his target. Alongside Sam Snead, Lee's swing just doesn't rate as picturebook stuff.

At the Lakes that week, Lee produced the most skilful variety of shots I had ever seen. He improvised, using imagination and finesse, and I realised that in teaching I had to do the same; that while the mechanics of the swing were relatively important, they were outweighed by the virtues of shot-making.

Doing television golf commentary for the Australian Broadcasting Commission has emphasised that point for me. That box seat gives one a very different view of a tournament and of those playing in it from the one the home viewer receives. For example, at the 1982 Australian Open I was able to see the inspiration Bob Shearer drew from playing with the great Jack Nicklaus, with his total concentration and professionalism.

I've told you about these men and events because I wanted to assure you that I don't spend my time merely tramping around golf courses. I thoroughly enjoy working with pupils who are willing to work to improve their game — a very satisfying occupation.

This book is designed to help you acquire the fruits of all those observations and practice of skills, techniques and approaches. Remember,

Lee Trevino

Jack Nicklaus

though, that you can never have them all. No one can. Trevino again:

God did not give everybody
  everything.
He withheld a short game from
  Nicklaus.
He kept back a soft shot from
  Watson's game.
Arnold Palmer was given everything
  but a brake pedal.
While Ben Hogan, who had
  everything else, also had an
  inconsistent putter.

I guess it is faults like these that help to make the game so exciting and yet so humbling. Golf is simple in its challenges, if not in its solutions.

There is no instant cure, no 'quick fix', for what ails your game. Rather, it is a matter of patience and hard work, reshaping your mental attitude and producing a gradual, steady progress, one stroke at a time.

To do that, the average or club player must get back to basics from time to time. The pros do it and there's a whole heap of advantages in you doing it, too. You will find continuing emphasis in this book on the fundamentals. The key is in knowing how and when to apply them.

Many ordinary players seem to believe that there is a secret to playing good golf—a secret the stars carefully keep to themselves. What nonsense! If ever a single secret existed then surely those thousands of hours of television coverage would have exposed it by now. And Jack Nicklaus wouldn't be going back to his old teaching professional each season to check the basics of his game. Nor would Lee Trevino be doing what he has always done: making the most of what he's got.

That, in a nutshell, is what I teach. Making the most of what you have can bring greater rewards than striving for the perfect swing. Concentrating on that ultimate ideal can, unfortunately, almost make you forget to get on with the game.

At first glance, golf is not a complex sport. Nor should it be. It becomes as complicated as we make it. That occasional golfer, Henry Ford, worked it out this way: 'Every difficult problem becomes easy to solve when you break it down into small ones, which are then taken one at a time'. Apply that theory to your golf and it all becomes beautifully simple.

Look at it this way. We get ourselves tied up in the mental acrobatics of trying to remember too many things about hitting the ball. We forget where we are going.

It is all about, first, aiming at and then, hitting to a target—nothing more or less than that. This is a completely natural action since, after all, part of man's basic instinct as a hunter is to hit a target. The next time you are in a park pick up a stone and side-arm throw it at some object. When you have done that the overwhelming problem of hitting a golf ball will have been broken down into three small problems:

You get set, you turn and you throw.

SET, TURN and THROW. **Three words to describe the golf swing.**

1. Take the address—get set (1A).
2. Swing back or pivot—turn (1B).
3. Strike the ball—throw (1C).

Think about it for a moment. The physical action involved in throwing the stone is a natural, almost automatic one. You don't think about throwing the stone; you are, in fact, concentrating on hitting the target.

Now, compare this scenario with that of hitting a golf ball—off a tee, for example.

If you are like most people, you will have concentrated on the physical side of swinging the club. You didn't give too much thought to your target, just a vague thought of getting it as far down the fairway as possible. In fact, the target was probably well down your list of things to remember.

Turn it all around. Concentrate on where you are going rather more than on what you are actually doing and the result could surprise you.

1A

1B

1C

Clearly, there are factors to remember within each individual part of the action of hitting a ball. We'll come to them properly in the following chapters. Basically, however, if you grip the club correctly, pivot your body the right way and strike the ball squarely, then you can take strokes off your score.

The secret is in having to remember as few of these factors as possible through developing muscle memory.

I don't believe the average golfer can keep more than two things in his mind at the same time as he's hitting a ball. The mistake most people make is in trying to recall too many things at once. Limit them. First and always is the need to keep your eye on the ball—not 'head down'. Then build your swing by adding one factor more each time, be it the grip, stance, backswing or whatever. In other words, start with the essentials and add on gradually.

All this, of course, means lots of practice, but the whole thing begins before you get anywhere near a golf course. First, you have to think about what you want out of golf, then set your goals and how you are going to achieve them. It's a sad truth that most of us pull back from admitting, but to be the best means you have to work at it every day. The place to start is inside your head.

It's been said many times that reading golf books doesn't make one a good golfer, and I suppose that is largely true. Yet, most books I have read offer sound advice for both beginners and potential improvers since they are a distillation of many years of experience by some pretty good players.

Not many, though, will tell you to be yourself and that is exactly what I want you to be. Henry Cotton put it this way: 'Merely copying out *Twelfth Night* doesn't make one a Shakespeare'.

Neither does copying Jack Nicklaus make you a Golden Bear.

Bobby Jones' swing was described as having 'all the drowsy beauty of a summer's day'. Well, that was fine for Bobby. But we can't all swing like that.

If yours has all the beauty of a man wielding a pickaxe, but it gets the ball to where you want it, then beauty has to take second place.

However, it is possible to learn much from watching stars like Nicklaus. I am thinking of the way in which he meticulously plans his round, deciding what he is going to do before he takes a club from his bag. Also, the way in which he takes his time, that deliberate oh-so-very Nicklaus backswing.

Another, quite different top-notcher to watch is Tom Watson. The tempo of his swing is brisk, yet it rarely alters.

Tempo and great concentration are also the hallmarks of Graham Marsh's game. He maintains that the biggest difference between the professional golfer and Mr Average is the latter's inability to maintain regular rhythm and extended concentration.

Without good tempo you cannot hope to feel where the club head is during the swing, the singularly most important factor in golf. You can learn from the stars—the combination of great finesse and awesome power make Greg Norman today's most exciting player. Just remember that each has his own individual rhythm and style, just as you have yours. Learn to make the most of them.

Greg Norman

Graham Marsh

2 Putting with Feeling

It may seem illogical to start out with the fundamentals of golf's short game, those shots taken from around the green. Yet, they are the scoring shots, the ones that matter the most.

A great drive off the tee or a long iron from the fairway can set up the likelihood of a par or even a birdie. But, unless you can finish off around and on the green, then much effort and a good shot is wasted.

Or to put it another way, a reliable short game can help you to recover from a poor drive. There are no club-players who can guarantee to hit a green every time. Even the touring professionals miss several greens in every round. But the reason for their consistent shooting of par or better is their short game—the trap play, the pitches, chips and putts that together make up 50 per cent of the game.

These shots do not need strength. Rather, they call for touch, judgement, skill and concentration. And yet these shots are the most under-practised in golf.

Any day on the practice fairway, I see the majority of club-players slamming away with a bucket of balls, using their drivers and long irons and virtually ignoring the finesse shots with nine-iron and wedge, let alone their putters. Then, later in the clubhouse, you hear them complaining about their poor short game!

I guess there is a nice, satisfying feeling about whacking a ball off into the blue somewhere, but force ten-type drives make up only a small part of any round. As Ben Hogan once said: 'The most important shot is your next one'.

And the most important part of any golf swing—in fact, the whole reason for it—is the moment of contact with the ball, that crucial point of impact.

Thus, when one stops and analyses all the strokes, it becomes apparent that there is a logical progression through the range.

Simply, there is an angle of descent for all clubs and all strokes. It starts with the softest shot, the putt, where the clubhead moves parallel to the ground and strikes the ball with a slightly rising blow.

Then you come to the tiny chipping shots, which brush the turf; the short irons pinching a divot; back to the long irons brushing the turf; and finally, the driver sweeping up the ball with a rising blow.

So, it is possible to see a very distinct arc with the clubs at either end of the range, the putter and driver, being very similar when the moment arrives for that point of contact with the ball.

Understanding this concept is the first step on the road to not only lower scores, but also to the discovery of a greater joy in the game itself.

'They make it look easy.' How many times have you said that to yourself when you've been watching the ABC's television coverages of the major golf events. Or the satellite pictures of the British Open and US Masters?

I'm talking of course about men like Nicklaus, Ballesteros, Norman, Palmer, Crenshaw, Trevino, Nagle, Marsh, Davis, Shearer and Watson—those who get down in two consistently. The difference between them and most golfers is that the pros make fewer errors. They also practise more, much more. After all it's their life and their business.

Taken all round, life for putters is better than it used to be. The way in which courses are prepared these days means that greens are smoother and softer than before the war. They are also more heavily grassed so that the approach shot to the green has a better chance of staying put somewhere near the flag.

Also, the bigger ball is easier to putt so that speed is more controllable. So, we are bound to see more one-putting than we used to, which is one reason why scores nowadays are a shade lower.

But what has this to do with you? Especially if your last round contained only a few 'getting down in twos'.

Standing over the ball with the cup only a metre or so away can be a nerve-wracking moment. Relax. And remember those immortal lines of Walter Hagen's: 'Don't hurry. Don't worry. You're only here for a short visit so don't forget to stop and smell the flowers'. In short, keep the pressure off yourself through clear thinking.

Walter Hagen was reckoned to have one of golf's finest putting touches, and I tell you this as a round-about way of emphasising that the art of putting is very much an individual thing, whatever the conditions, whatever the era.

There are, however, a few salient points common to the putting styles of the latter-day Hagens. One of them is the naturalness in the stroke. And most of them, you will find, do not forget to put their trust on the putting green in their right hands. Even Bob Shearer with his cross-handed technique—which is a variation on keeping the wrists firm and putting with the arms—relies on his right hand.

A common misunderstanding I've found is the belief held by many golfers that putting is a left-handed *only* business. That's wrong. It's a two-handed game. Listen to people who are putting badly and nine times out of ten they will say that their clumsy right hand is getting in the way of successful putting.

In putting, I like to feel that the left hand holds the club with just a slight touch of firmness. It is the right hand that is doing the job of finding touch, just as it does in almost everything. Play snooker and billiards and it's the left hand which forms the bridge, the smart right hand does the tricky stuff. Write a letter, pluck a hair from your eye; in any delicate task the right hand is relied on naturally to do the skilful part of any task.

Try it for yourself at putting practice. Keep the left arm behind your back and use the right. Then reverse the procedure and decide for yourself which hand is the easiest to use and is the most accurate.

The task now is to train the right hand and arm to do the correct thing on the putting green; working in conjunction with the left, just like dancing partners.

As in any sport, perfection comes from not merely practice, but from *intelligent* practice. Don't do the same thing so many times that you become bored and defeat the whole purpose of the exercise. Later, I will show you different ways to do this, but for now, experiment with different putting styles and grip pressures, until you find the combination that is best suited to you and your game.

THE GRIP

About 60 per cent of the touring pros use the reverse overlap grip for putting and because they do, it is known as the standard grip.

To begin, the palms of both hands should be parallel to the face of the club. The shaft sits in the middle of the left palm with the thumb directly down the shaft. It should also be held in the middle of the right palm. The forefinger of the left hand then overlaps one or two fingers of the right (1A–E).

Greg Norman uses the conventional reverse overlap grip, and states that his right arm is the control factor in his super technique 'à la Crenshaw'.

Generally, grip pressures vary enormously, but in general they should be light, yet flexible.

You must experiment to find the correct pressure for you, but please keep in mind that the left hand is the holder, the right is the doer or the skilful one.

1A

1B

1C

1D

1E

GRIP VARIATIONS

From time to time you will find some of the leading players trying out variations in their putting grips, seeking greater touch in their strokes. Mostly, it is not their grip which is the main reason for any falling away in their putting standards, rather the ways in which they are executing the stroke.

Occasionally, however, a change in style brings greater rewards, as it did when Bob Shearer moved to a cross-handed grip which, effectively, is a mirror-image of the orthodox reverse overlap. Note though that it is his right hand which still does the skilful stuff in holing putts. American Bruce Leitzke also favours this grip; both he and Shearer pull the putter through instead of pushing (2A).

The axe or baseball grip is split-handed in that there is a gap showing in the leather between the forefinger of the left hand and the pinkie of the right (2B). It looks awkward, but obviously it works. Art Wall has used this style, so too did Dai Rees the great Welsh champion, and Sir Donald Bradman, who played off scratch at Kooyonga Club in Adelaide.

Additionally, there is the double overlap grip, with the little finger per-

2A

2B

2C

forming this task (2C). Gary Player has used it, as has Graham Marsh, especially back in the early 1970s when his putting had not yet taken on the confidence and authority it now possesses.

Try the various styles if you wish but once you have developed a grip that is comfortable and suited to you, then trust it!

Probably the last step down the line in putting grips is one taught, used and recommended by the American golf teacher, Paul Runyan, for that dreaded time when a golfer's sense of touch has all but departed. The great Sam Snead developed his now-famous sidesaddle style a few years ago, for this situation.

Simply, it is a lock-wristed grip where both hands are twisted underneath the clubshaft so that the palms face upwards. The wrists are directly opposed with the thumbs on the forward and rear sides of the shaft.

You are forced to putt with your elbows and shoulders, virtually eliminating the hands and wrists, which the golfer who uses this grip probably has come to distrust. That is the odd thing about it and just shows how psychological putting can be.

Golfers who turn to this grip still manage to do other skilful things with their hands. Yet when they take hold of the putter they have usually psyched themselves out of the stroke and are looking for some magic formula.

Well, there is a formula but it has more to do with getting back to putting basics than with magic.

THE KEY ELEMENTS

There are two key elements in putting; the remainder is technique, style and concentration.

The first element is the size of the putting blade.

The other is the size of the ball.

The blade is surprisingly shallow, about half the size of the ball. You will see this if you hold the putter blade at eye-level and place the middle of the ball against the middle of the blade.

That is where the ball has to be struck and for correct contact to be made, the bottom of the blade has to be a centimetre above the ground.

So, all those people who make practice swings with their putter brushing the turf are wasting their time. The blade is too low and, in truth, they are rehearsing to strike the ball in the wrong place. It will track with a backspin skid, making it susceptible in the first metre or so of travel to deflection from any faint indentation in the ground, such as spike marks.

However, if the ball is struck in its centre with the middle, or even the bottom of the blade, it will track with a topspin effect, making it *less* susceptible to deflection.

Striking with the bottom of the blade is a good fault to have, for it means the ball is being hit on the upswing. Many top golfers, such as Trevino and Nicklaus, deliberately putt in this way to get overspin into the early part of the putt and make the ball track more truly.

A method I use in teaching people to putt a good line is to take one of those range practice balls with the red stripes. Use it in your putting practice and you will see that it is like a red wheel vertically aligned to the target. Strike incorrectly and those red lines will wobble all over the place. Hit truly with a little overspin and those red lines will roll towards the cup like a wheel.

THE STANDARD PUTTING STROKE

The stance should be comfortably erect (3A); in this way it is much easier to look down along the line you intend to putt. There should be a slight slouch to the shoulders; the knees bent but relaxed; the elbows

3A

comfortably spread and the palms parallel to each other in one of the grips illustrated. Comfort in the stance is the important factor.

The eyes are directly over the ball, from both front and side elevations, enabling you to sight along the putting line and ensure that the putting blade is square (3B, C).

Interestingly, Nicklaus varies this method. He takes his address with his head directly over the ball from the side view, but when seen from the front, his head is well behind the ball. He uses the same stance in chipping, which has been a relatively indifferent part of his game over the years. In putting, however, the advantage in having his head over the right foot (i.e. behind the ball) is that he is able to stroke the ball slightly on the upswing, thus imparting topspin.

That factor in Nicklaus' approach also fits in with the theory that the right hand on the putter is the controlling force. Being behind the ball in the stance makes him feel more comfortable in stroking and pushing through the ball.

At the Australian Open in Sydney in 1982, he told me that this is getting back to the feeling he used to have some years ago when he was putting very well, that the right arm is the delivery arm.

When putting, it is just as important as in any other stroke to collect the ball in the 'sweet spot' of the blade. Correct timing of the stroke can come from only one place, exactly in the centre, horizontally and vertically.

For centre, there should be a mark denoting this on top of the putter blade. If there isn't, a pencil mark or even a small hacksaw cut will do the same job.

Horizontally, the 'sweet spot' is centred between heel and toe of the 'ping'-type clubs which I prefer, as

3B

3C

do Tom Watson and Seve Ballesteros. This type has a slightly wider 'sweet spot' than the stock blade putter used by Nicklaus.

So, the four ways in which you can mistime a shot are apparent:

Off-centre either way.

Too high on the blade.

Too low.

Only one of these is effective. Catching the ball low on the blade at least imparts overspin and it is the only type of mistimed contact which can make the ball go full distance. So, if you are going to be wrong, you will be less wrong by being above the centre of the ball a fraction.

TECHNIQUES

There are not many wrist putters playing the game today. In the old days of golf, everyone was wristy in their technique and I don't know if the change has been for the good or not. Bobby Jones was the star then and I wouldn't be surprised to see an old-fashioned wrist stylist coming along and holing everything in sight over the next few years, and then it will all change back again.

Palmer and Casper used to be great wrist putters, but styles altered with the trend towards a firm push with the arms and a minimum of wrist movement. For this style, watch Ben Crenshaw. He is the epitome of modern putters.

The technique is one of being near to stiff arm, keeping the hand action down to the point where there is just enough to supply feel. For beginners, I believe it to be the best and certainly the safest method of putting. Later, they can experiment. If we stop and think about it, putting revolves around a sense of touch, and if you can develop it by using your wrists, then that is the style for you.

If you do wish to experiment, then do it on the practice green or at home on the lounge-room carpet. First try it single-handed, left then right; when you put both hands on the putter, there are five basic combinations of technique to try.

1. The stroke is controlled completely with the left hand.
2. You can take the club back and through with both hands.
3. Control the club with the right hand.
4. Back with the right arm and through with the left.
5. Take the club back with the left arm and through with the right arm. That's the way the great South African, Bobby Locke, putted, and he was a master.

The basic factors in your experimentation are: which hand or arm is the dominant force and whether you use all arm or all wrist, or a combination.

But I stress again, that putting technique is an individual matter in the end, and it doesn't matter which one you settle on, provided it is the best for you.

With all styles, however, there are very few successful putters who move their bodies. From the waist down and from the neck up, there is no movement; any in between must be smooth and at a minimum.

TOUCH FOR DISTANCE

Your touch depends upon on how you accelerate through the ball in the putting stroke. A smooth, firm push gives the best results day in and day out.

If you have a short, jerky, stabbing action, you will find it difficult to judge distance in the putt, as did Roger Stephens, the young Australian professional.

The problem was cured by getting Roger to tie an old fishing sinker at the bottom of half a metre of string, and the other end of the string around his right forefinger. I get other pupils to do the same. The idea is that they take their putting grip on the club and swing back and forth, trying to keep the string and the shaft parallel. That produces minimum acceleration for it is gravity working, making a true pendulum stroke. That pendulum speed is the slowest you can swing and still be a good putter. Anything slower and you won't be able to putt for nuts. If you get too quick, then you start to lose your touch, so somewhere in between is the ideal tempo of the stroke.

As I will later suggest with pitching and chipping, the best way to adjust for distance is to shorten or lengthen the backstroke in the putting movement.

For increased length, take a longer backstroke so that you can accelerate a fraction faster through the ball. For less distance, shorten the backswing so that the acceleration is not as sharp.

No doubt, you have heard of the term, 'yips'. It is used to describe—and very vividly too—the state of being in the putting horrors. Golfers with the 'yips' can't do anything right. Generally, they have a short backstroke for any kind of putt and consequently hit the ball hard to compensate. They don't hole out, they miscue, heel the ball, toe the ball, do everything wrong. And the more they keep doing things wrongly, the more the errors compound themselves. Perhaps the best-known case of the 'yips' in recent years belonged to Peter Alliss. A promising tournament player and British representative, Peter finally gave up the circuit to concentrate on writing and commenting on golf for the major world television networks. And all because of horrible affliction which is more psychological than anything else.

Physically, the way to get out of the 'yips' is to do what I suggested with the sinker and string, getting back the feeling of the putter head with a smooth rhythmical stroke. Once you recover the sense of rolling the ball to the cup, rather than hitting it, you will be well on your way back to normal putting and the enjoyment of it. Naturally, it takes a lot of work, mentally and physically.

HOLING SPEEDS

The average golfer is ten times worse at judging length than he is at judging direction. Only training can sharpen that perception, which is the most crucial part of developing into a good putter.

If a putt doesn't travel far enough, you have to ask yourself two questions:

1. Did I misjudge the distance?
2. Or, did I mistime the ball?

If the latter, then you must concentrate on contacting the ball at the correct height with the putter's 'sweet spot' in a smooth, accelerating stroke.

If the former, then the best way to work out the problem is on the practice green.

The ideal holing speed for a putt is just enough to nudge the back of the cup to let the ball fall in. That is, if the ball missed it should stop somewhere between the back of the cup and twenty-two to thirty centimetres beyond it.

That is the holing speed you have to practise.

Place a tee-peg in the ground thirty centimetres past the hole and set out a line of six to eight balls at about half-metre intervals and roll them up to the hole (4A). Don't necessarily try to hole them, but concentrate on achieving that ideal speed. If your speed is correct, then all the balls should finish in that area between the cup and the tee-peg. Move back along the line, starting with the ball nearest the hole, and with each, stroke a little longer, a little more firmly until you can get the right speed for each length of putt.

Once you have used all the balls, mark the spot where you played your last putt, pick up the balls and go

4A

back working even further away from the hole, until you are about twenty-five metres away. Think solely of timing the ball in the 'sweet spot' and achieving a smooth acceleration.

When you've hit the last in the string of putts, pace it off and recognise how far away you were. The distances will soon register on the brain's memory banks.

On the golf course, too, you are entitled to walk along your line of putt to clear leaves and other debris.

On the way back to your ball, quietly count off the paces, which will give you an idea of the distance involved in the putt.

Not many golfers do this, which is why they seem to have trouble when they get into three-putt territory anywhere within twenty-five paces of the cup. And that amazes me. They will be able to tell you they were exactly 127 paces for their second shot to the green, but are less than meticulous when it comes to putting distances.

Another exercise aimed at developing your correct holing speed is to spread a circle of balls around a hole (4B). This time, concentrate on trying to hole them, hitting with enough speed to nudge the back of the cup. This approach lets you develop holing speeds over different parts of the green, with differing slopes and undulations.

Once you achieve consistency in being able to stop the ball in that area behind the cup, you will also have become consistent in reading the line to the hole.

If you dead-pace the ball, it will take maximum borrow; if you run it a metre past the cup, the ball will not have enough borrow. Unless you are

4B

aware of the fact that **too hard means not enough borrow, and too soft means maximum borrow**, then you are inclined to adjust your aim, when it is pace you should be adjusting.

Become consistent with timing and length and you will find that getting your line will become much easier. Adjust pace first, then aim or line.

READING THE GREEN

A good approach before putting is to visualise the hole at the centre end of a metre-wide footpath and look half a metre each side of the hole to see which side is the high one. So scan across your line, not just along it. The faster the green, the more borrow.

Every putt you will ever hit is a straight putt, no matter how much bend you know is there. To illustrate the point, I have placed an orange ball on Royal Melbourne's Sixth Green about six paces above the hole (5A). That is the amount of borrow I estimate the ball will need to curve to the cup; it is the aiming point on the shoulder of the line.

Before putting, I visualise a solid straight line to that point, allowing for the bend and the natural slope to take the ball to the hole.

Again, the curved line of balls shows in another way how the putt will have gravity exerted on it. The essential point is that I am putting in a straight line above the hole to the estimated shoulder (5B).

So, every putt is a straight one—the club swinging straight back and through towards the target point.

Before settling down to make the stroke, always remember that your *second* last look should be at the hole. The *last* look is at the target point—visualise the straight line to that and stroke the ball directly to it.

5B

5A

PRACTICE

It is vital to practise the mechanics of your putting, but there are other equally important aspects of this part of golf that require time spent on them.

Practising these will expand your mental horizons towards the game. In short, you have to make yourself think about what you are doing. You can do this by working out on the practice green in various ways. Reading the borrow of the green, groom your holing speeds from various distances, up slopes, down and across slopes, making and developing putting decisions to ready you for the real thing out on the course.

There are also quick, corrective measures for when the putts aren't going right. For example, if your line is off, maybe it is because you have wandered away from taking the correct stance; your eyes are not over the ball and putter blade.

Check this by holding the club between thumb and forefinger under your chin (6A). Let it hang above the ball and check your eye-level for correctness.

6A

If you have discovered that a wristy style does not suit, yet have allowed a wristiness to develop in your style, a simple way to train the left wrist to stay firm is to place a comb on the wrist, held there by your watchband (6B).

Whatever the problems, the practice green is the place to sort them out, so take the time to identify basic faults and work on your putting patterns.

The most brilliant putter I have seen was Bobby Locke. It was the feature of his game, and it made him one of the best golfers of his time. He could be counted on to hole more putts than anyone else.

6B

The secret to Bobby's putting was his immense power of concentration, and over the years, he distilled it all down to one simple thought . . .

Hit the ball in the middle of the blade and do not move the eyes until the ball is out of sight.

To which I might add: focus on the back of the ball and after it has been stroked, keep looking at where the ball was.

Probably the epitome of this was Guy Wolstenholme. A very good putter, Guy looked down and kept looking down almost to the point of exaggeration. He let the ball get almost to the hole before he looked up to see where it had gone. Even then, he did not straighten up and turn his head. He followed the putt only by rotating his head and eyes, in fact maintaining his follow-through position for many seconds.

Guy was a good example of what Bobby Locke believed—that after sorting out line and length, the putter concentrates on timing and stroking the ball properly and then lets it get out of sight.

I cannot think of two finer examples of the art of putting.

The Crater Hole

ELEVENTH, ROYAL ADELAIDE GC

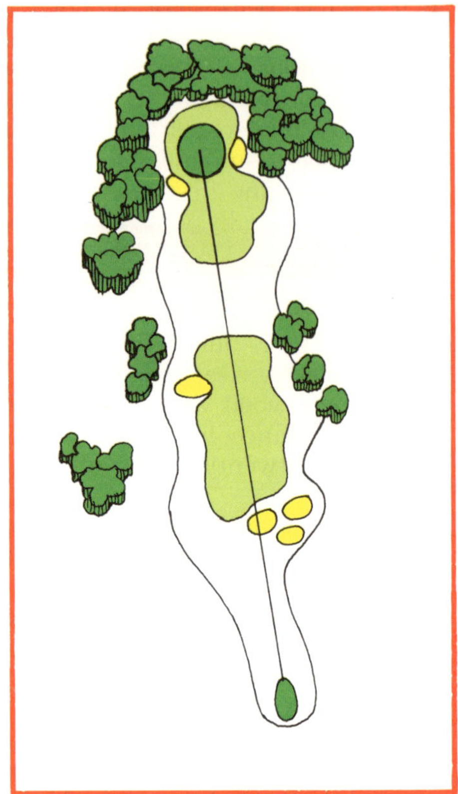

This would be a good time to give an example of how the average man and woman would play a hole.

Daughter Jane and I approach the task set by the Eleventh at Royal Adelaide in much the same way, but conditions between tee and green highlight what differences there are in men's and women's techniques.

The Eleventh is a small pocket of Royal Adelaide, one of the most demanding championship layouts in the country because of its sand, hillocks and changing wind patterns. It was built in the early part of this century; but through modern re-designs it now bears the stamp of Dr Alistair McKenzie (who did the major part of his work about the same time as he did Royal Melbourne) and Peter Thomson.

Together, they have made Royal Adelaide into a mighty good course, and by design or not, thick marram grass and the sand dunes add to its character.

The Eleventh, or the Crater Hole as it is called because of the bowl in which the green lies, is a medium-length par four—355 metres for the men, 305 for the ladies.

The hole 'reads' easily enough from the tee. The requirement for men is to drive over the first fairway rise; the women usually would be on or about that.

With the aid of a sea-breeze tailwind, my drive has landed slightly right of centre, but well up on the second fairway rise. Jane, trying out a new metalwood with a long shaft for extra distance, has placed her tee shot about twenty paces short of mine.

Each of us has open shots to the green; mine is about 140 paces with a six-iron, while Jane has chosen the five. Don't forget that tailwind—Jane hasn't, and aims to take advantage of it with extra height off that fairway rise.

Just as Mr and Miss Average would probably play this hole, both of us are slightly short of the green. My lie is in a sandy waste, with a trap between the shot and the pin. Jane is just off to the right in a shallow depression. Her pitch with the wedge runs the ball up to the cup for a par putt. I use the sand iron for a loose-wristed flip shot over that bunker and get the ball up half a metre past the cup, also enough for a par.

For the club-player, man and woman, our approaches to the Eleventh would be about normal, making the Crater a probable par for anyone who thinks about what they are doing. But the ways in which Jane and I played between tee and green point up the slight differences between men and women golfers. Women tend to sweep through their drives, while men usually have greater strength in their arms and wrists.

Thus Jane's drives normally will carry less distance, but closer to the green is where a balance will be struck.

A Stroke Player's Hole

SEVENTH, THE AUSTRALIAN GC, SYDNEY—PAR FOUR, 382 METRES

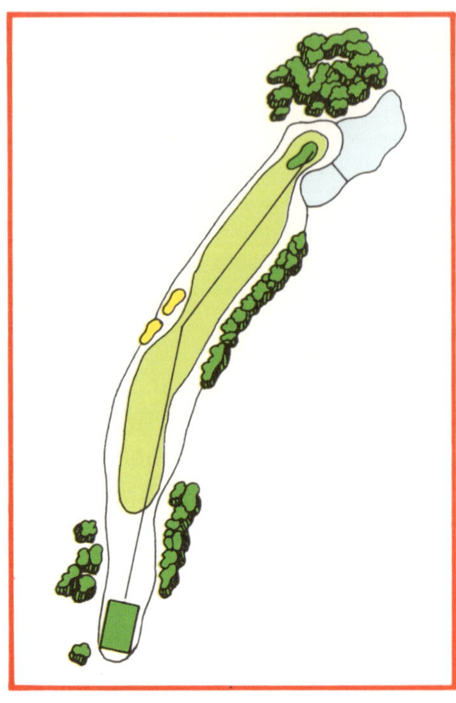

Darrell Welch is the resident professional at the Australian Club in Sydney. He calls it a long and straight hitter's course.

Still, when Jack Nicklaus redesigned the layout in the mid-70s, he didn't neglect the greens. Darrell describes them as fast, but not to the same degree as Royal Melbourne's.

The Seventh is a fair example of most of the holes on the Australian layout—hard but fair to all, provided the line for all shots is straight. Any attempt to fade or draw can be dangerous.

With the prevailing wind left to right, tee up on the right-hand side to aim left of the fairway. Sandtraps here will put pressure on the drive, so it is wise to be slightly short.

From this point, the Seventh gets harder particularly with the breeze now coming from over the left shoulder for the second shot.

The five-iron from here must not be short because of the pond in front of the right-hand side of the green.

That pond also skirts the rear, so neither must the shot be long. It is obviously very penal to any but the most accurate second shot. Aim for somewhere between the mounds and the flag on the left-hand side of the green. If in doubt, lay up a short for two and rely on your chip shot to make par or, at worst, a five.

As Darrell says about this hole, the rolling, elongated green really tests the player's putting mettle. It is a three-tiered affair, and on this day, the flag is set back on the rear step. For the putt like this one, which is up and over the step, read the borrow as you would normally, but add a metre to the usual length. A deceptively tough hole.

A Small Alteration

FOURTEENTH, ROYAL MELBOURNE COMPOSITE—PAR FIVE, 446 METRES

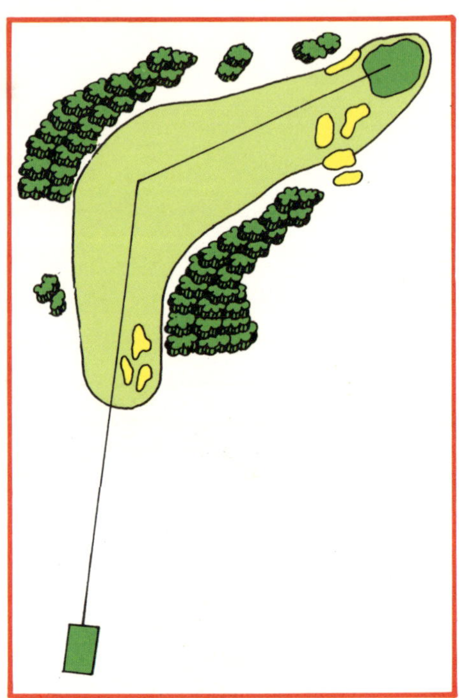

All over the world, many clubs, it seems, can't resist changing their layouts. Royal Melbourne, on the other hand, could hardly improve on what Dr Alistair McKenzie and Alex Russell gave it back in the '20s and '30s.

Their legacy is superb couch fairways, deep bunkering and fast, true greens. How could anyone improve on the best? This is a case that can be argued with conviction. So, when the Royal Melbourne Council did make a change in 1979–80, the decision came only after lengthy debate and much agonising. Not that the alteration was major, but it was significant.

The tee at the Composite Fourteenth was moved back sixteen metres. (More correctly, it is the West Course Fourth Hole. But for the Australian PGA Championship, and television coverage of that event, the hole is the Fourteenth.)

The effect of this decision has been to make the hole more stimulating, both visually and as a test of golf. It turned the Fourteenth from what Peter Thomson called 'one of the world's great par fours' into an even better par five, and increased par for the composite layout to 72.

Before the change, the Fourteenth averaged 4·5 strokes during the Australian PGA event. Since then, the birdies have been a little easier to obtain by the pros, but only if they play it perfectly.

For the average club member at Royal Melbourne, the hole can be a delight. It demands a solid drive from the new tee out over fairway bunkers slightly right of centre; then a fairway wood, perhaps slightly faded around the right-hand bend (one could hardly call it a dog-leg), with the approach to be made to the left side and finally, a wedge over the bunker guarding that side of the green.

Putting is, well—it's not easy. It never is at the Royal. But any player who is patient and in control of his temperament will get down in two.

Odd, isn't it, how there is one hole on every championship course which seems to provide the turning point in a tournament? The Fourteenth fills that role at Royal Melbourne, and more money and titles have been won and lost from there than I care to remember.

It's a pleasure to be on the green at the Seventh at the Australian, both for the beautiful surroundings and the comfort of having avoided the lake.

3 The Short Game

Your golf game can only be as sound as the total sum of its parts; a weakness in any stroke will lessen that soundness. It is equally true that each part of the body has its role in actually hitting the ball. Working together, they produce the force and the control necessary to play good golf. It happens this way:

1. The feet, legs and hips produce the initial driving force in the swing.
2. Shoulders and arms are the second stage, building up on the force ignited by the body's lower half.
3. Finally, from the hands come the acceleration and control over the clubhead.

When all these parts are put together the result is what I call the 'cartwheel effect'.

Imagine, if you will, that the body is the hub of the wheel which drives the rim or, in effect, the clubhead (1). The body, coiling and uncoiling, whips the clubhead through. The reason why many people do not get force into their swing is because the clubhead is actually driving the body or, if you like, the rim is driving the hub, which is of course not the way a wheel works. **The hub must drive the rim.**

The full turn of the wheel (the complete swing of the clubhead) is the full-blooded shot. For something less, the clubhead only travels, say, three-quarters of the circle. The short game, therefore, involves a swing of the clubhead through only half or less of the swing involved in the full shot.

1

By definition, any good golf shot requires accuracy and distance. That means control and a level of force.

In the short game, the level of force is low, but the control factor is high, and there is only one way to get it—through the hands. They have to work as a single unit. If they do not, you can't get the clubhead to do what you want it to do.

It starts with the grip. Get the grip right and you have taken one of the most important steps towards playing better golf. If your present game is ailing then it's a good idea to get back to checking the fundamentals, especially the grip.

The hands have to hold the club with enough tension to prevent it from getting away from you, or from twisting so that the face is at the wrong angle at the moment of striking the ball. At the same time, they must not be so tight that all the tension they are producing flows back through the body, throwing everything else out of rhythm.

The secret lies in the fingers, the most sensitive parts of the hands. That brings us back to that theme of likening the action of striking the ball to that of throwing a stone. You feel the club shaft, just as you did the stone, through the fingers. Your hands must be strong and yet have the touch required by a master billiards or snooker champion.

For all golf shots, the importance of the grip lies in its intent, which is simply to enable you to transfer your speed and skill to the clubhead. To do this efficiently, the grip must be of a kind that will allow the hands and wrists to work together, left and right. The one I teach for all shots except the putt is the overlap grip which I have found suits a high percentage of people. It is called the Vardon grip.

Until it becomes second nature to you, it is important to follow the routine of getting it right. In setting up, first place the clubhead on the ground square to the target line. Doing this will help to ensure that the clubface is in that position when it contacts the ball through the swing.

In taking the grip, both palms are parallel to each other and, in turn, parallel to the clubface.

FIRST, THE LEFT HAND

Place the top of the shaft at the bottom corner of the left palm (2A). It runs slightly diagonally across the palm to the large knuckle of the index finger just above the pad of the hand (2B).

With the hand closed, the thumb will be on top of or slightly to the right of the shaft and you should be able to see two, and possibly three, knuckles (2C).

Pressure in the left hand comes in the last two or three fingers, rather than in the thumb or index finger (2D). The reason for this is that at the top of the swing this area comes under a good deal of pressure. A common error is to let go at the top of the swing then re-grip, resulting in the clubface being twisted at the moment of the impact.

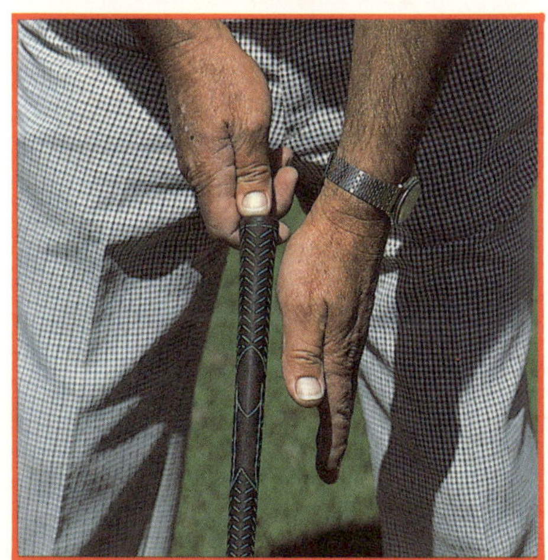
2A

2B

2C

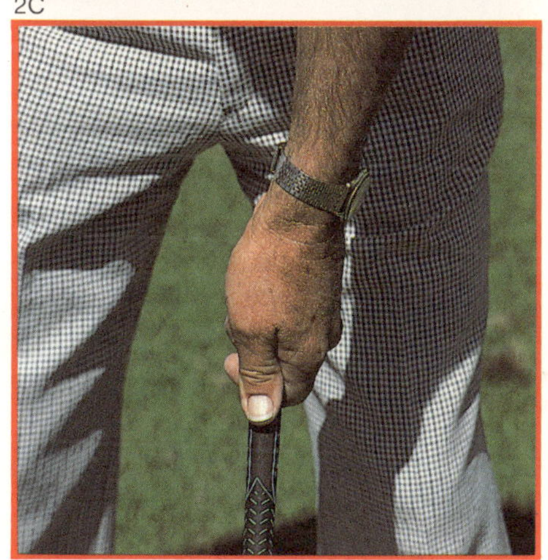
2D

NEXT, THE RIGHT HAND

It comes in parallel with the face of the club, the wrist arched slightly downwards and the clubshaft running through the groove of the fingers as they close (3A). The thumb is placed slightly forward of the shaft and pressure exerted through the index and second fingers, slightly less through the thumb. Basically, what you have is the grip you would use to hold a ball and throw it.

Now, the overlapping part of the grip comes with the little finger of the right hand sitting just behind the knuckle of the left index finger (3B). This serves to slightly strengthen the left hand and slightly weaken the right.

The left hand should grip the club to about 50 per cent of maximum pressure and the right hand about 30 per cent.

One very good way of checking the grip is in a mirror. You will see the vees formed by the thumbs and forefingers running away slightly to the right of centre, pointing somewhere between your nose and right ear (3C).

3A

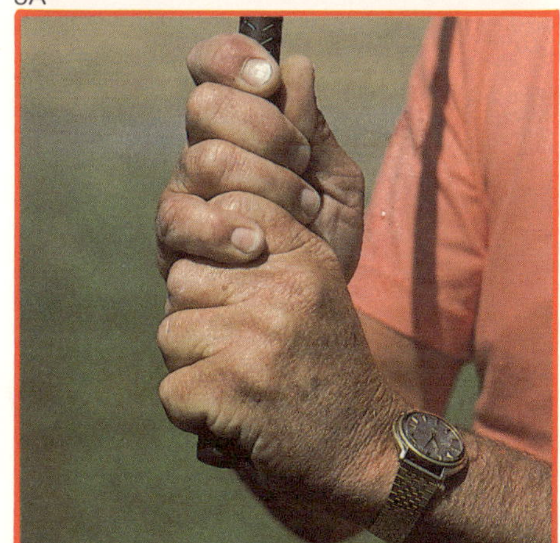
3B

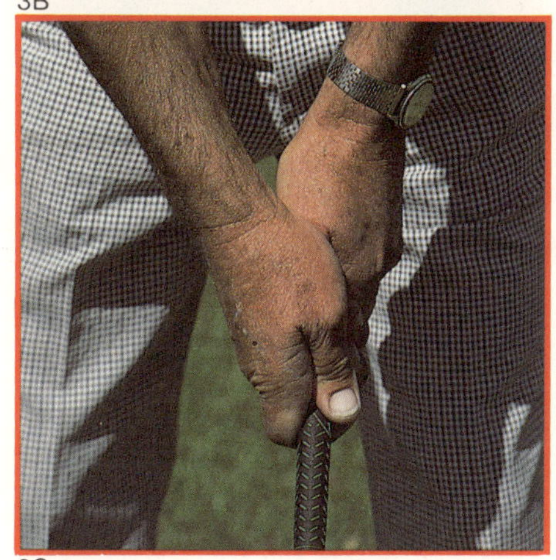
3C

The grip is a neutral one, neither a slicer's grip nor a hooker's. With it, you are able to mould your hands together as one unit and be better able to manipulate the clubhead.

There is a variation of this basic grip for people with either small hands or stout fingers. Simply intertwine the forefinger and little finger together into an interlocking grip. It's one used by Jack Nicklaus (3D).

Another is useful for children or women with small hands. This is the baseball or eight-finger grip as used by top US professional, Beth Daniel. Merely set the clubshaft into the hands as you would for the basic grip, but do not overlap the fingers (3E).

If you do have small hands and find that neither variation really suits, it's worth trying thinner grips on your clubs. Your local pro will do the change-over for you and enable you to use the basic overlap grip.

3D

3E

CHECKING THE GRIP

To ensure the correct grip, raise the club to waist-height, checking that the clubface is still square (as it was, sitting on the ground at the start of the drill). If your hands look twisted one way or the other, then start again. You should feel, in fact, that you are shaking hands with the club—both hands.

For that problem of the fingers flying open at the top of the swing, here's an exercise to cure it. Swing one-handed for just a few minutes each day, first with the left hand, then with the right. You will soon learn to grip the club with the correct pressure on the correct fingers and, at the same time, strengthen them. A sand iron is the best club to use in this routine because of its weight. Nicklaus often starts his warm-up drill in this way.

Another common grip error is to hold the club in the middle of the right palm, instead of with the fingers. With this, the right hand is underneath the shaft, virtually in a fist-like grip. It gives an impression of strength but in reality is the wrong application of power. The wrist becomes locked as in a punching action and you lose the flexibility needed to make the proper golf shot. The grip must be in the fingers with the palm facing the target.

If the grip with the right hand is correct, then your right elbow will be down and pointing in towards your right hip, thus keeping the right shoulder down at the address. You've no doubt seen the pros addressing the ball in this way and now you know that it all begins with the proper grip on the club. In a nutshell:

Pressure: Hold the club with the Vardon grip, applying about 50 per cent of your maximum pressure through the left hand, and about 30 per cent through the right. The left hand is the guiding hand, while the right is the power hand that will throw the clubhead through the ball.

With his distinctive way of expressing things, Trevino puts it this way: 'The left hand is the horse, the right hand is the cart. There's no point in giving instructions to the cart, is there?'

Vees: The lines formed by the thumbs and forefingers must point in the same direction, usually just to the right of a line past your nose.

The Hands: Their job is to return the clubhead to the point of impact square to the target and at the speed you have decided is required to reach your target. The key lies in the fingers and the touch they give to the individual shot.

PITCHING AND CHIPPING

I had better say here and now that pitching and chipping make up one of the least understood arts of golf.

Average and occasionally better players who, at least for some of the time, know their way around with the driver and long iron, can succumb to a fit of the horrors when it comes to playing the softer shot.

Usually, they make any of five everyday errors. Frequently, it's a combination of the lot.

Let's look at these DON'TS at the outset.

1. HOOKING

Hood the club blade at the address and I guarantee you will hook, which, for 99 per cent of the time, is exactly what you don't want in pitching shots. It means the blade is twisted slightly to the left of the target, encouraging the ball to run excessively.

Far better to open the clubface slightly, say about 5 degrees or more. This helps to cut the ball, slice it a little bit to the right and increase not only the backspin and height but also your control over the shot.

2. INCORRECT BODY WEIGHT

I often see people setting behind the ball on the right leg at the address when they should be keeping their weight on the left.

The correct amount of weight to place on the left leg at the address is about 70 per cent. Start out balanced about 50-50 on each leg then add a slight lean to the left, and keep it there right throughout the swing.

A good way of checking is to hold the club between thumb and forefinger and let it hang from just below your chin. The shaft should be level with the front edge of the ball or a little beyond.

Incidentally, this business of weight is one reason why Nicklaus has been a relatively indifferent chipper for much of his career. He doesn't set his head and neck over or in front of the ball. His body weight is more on the left leg, right enough, but his head is *behind* the ball.

If the average golfer does this and adds to the problem by placing his weight on the right leg instead of the left, then you can understand why so many people have trouble with the softer shots.

However, the point cannot be made in isolation, for it is related to the spot from where you are playing the ball.

3. BALL PLACEMENT

A lot of golfers nowadays believe that all pitches should be played with the ball in line with the left heel. They believe this because they have watched many top professionals not only do it, but also advise everybody else to do it.

This particular shot is fine if what you are looking for is a high-flyer from a good lie. Yet, how many of those do you get? If you are a top pro, you are likely to get plenty since most championship courses are well-manicured and you want to get excessive flight into the shot so that the ball will stop more quickly.

On the average Australian course, particularly the public ones, lies for the pitch are not so good and the ball generally will sit down snugly into the grass. Another reason for the leading players striking their pitches off the left heel is that most of them have a very strong, fast-driving leg action, which the average person does not have. The pros also know the knack of delaying their wrist action so that they can collect the ball properly off the left heel.

It is one of the few points on which I find myself in disagreement with these players.

What you should be aiming for is to play, and play well, the standard or stock pitching shot with the ball played off the centre, equi-distant between the two feet. With the ball in the centre, and not off the left heel, you can collect the ball just *before* or *at* the lowest point of your swing, just brushing it off the turf. Thus, the shot is a more controllable one and consequently, more reliable in the long run.

Obviously, there is a place for the pitch played with the ball off the left heel, but it requires many hours of practice.

4. SWING

Pitching means lobbing the ball in to the green from a point anywhere between twenty-five to 100 paces out. Clearly, the shot does not call for a full-blooded swing.

Yet, it is interesting to see how the average golfer approaches the problem. He tends to make a full-backswing, then decelerates the clubhead as it comes down to the ball, producing a jerky sort of shot, neither one thing nor the other, with little or no control.

Acceleration is the secret. If the club is taken back no more than shoulder-high, then accelerated down, properly and smoothly, you will make good contact with the ball. If the shot doesn't go far enough, simply add a little more to the backswing. If the ball goes too far, don't hit it more softly; shorten the backstroke, but still accelerate smoothly.

Backswing and acceleration must be in balance. As I said, the average fellow takes the club back too far, then quits half-way through the shot.

5. PLAYING 'UP'

What a misleading word 'up' is! In most ball sports, the main thought is getting the ball to the target.

In golf, the aim *seems* to be 'get the ball up in the air', then worry about the direction, which, of course, is the wrong way round.

Unfortunately for most beginners, the first thing they do is top the ball which immediately plants the thought that they must get the ball 'up'. That germ of a thought stays with them and when it comes to pitching, they work their wrists trying to flick the ball into the air. Obviously, there is a place for this kind of shot, but it is an extremely dangerous one that needs to be mastered through hours of practice.

In pitching, don't let yourself go back and up. Hit down and forward, making the clubhead do the work. If the choice of club is correct, the blade will do the work and there will be no need for that risky flick with the wrists.

THINKING AND PLANNING

Now, I did say there were five basic errors with the pitch. In truth, there is a sixth: lack of forethought about a shot.

First of all, look at the ball's lie in relation to the green and ask yourself how much loft will the ball need? How much run over the green will it require? If your shot is one of about fifty paces, the club selection for it will depend upon two main factors:

1. Is there a wind which is likely to affect the ball? If so, from which

direction? If it's a headwind, then you won't be pitching the ball up high, and the club will have to be an eight or nine-iron to keep it down.

2. How many hazards are there between you and the flagstick? There could be several undulations or sharp bunkers in front of the green. With the eight-iron, the ball should be struck about thirty-five paces, then run fifteen more. With the wedge, it will lob forty-five paces away from you and run the other five. The more loft used, the more risky the shot, but sometimes the wedge has to be the club chosen because of the hazards in front of the green.

It is a matter of intelligent observation of the conditions and the answers to the questions they pose will govern how successful the pitch will be.

DISTANCE

Pitching is, you will recall, the bottom half of the full swing arc, or, if you like, the cartwheel. Clubs for the shot range from the eight through to the wedge. The eight or nine are pretty good pitching clubs when the approach to the green is flat. If the ball has to carry, then stop quickly, choose the wedge or the sand iron.

Finding the range with all of them is not as difficult as some people believe. The first piece of knowledge to have is how far you can hit a ball with a full swing with each of them. From that point, it is a matter of progression.

Let's take the nine-iron, for example. I know what distance I can get with it: about 120 paces. So, if the pitch facing me is one of about sixty paces, I know that the shot will require only a half-swing with half-force. Yet, as in all these shots, the clubhead must be accelerating smoothly.

Knowing what distance you can get with each club places you into the position of adjusting your swing and force for the lesser distances. The issue is one of feeling and adjustment, but the formula is a simple one.

For a half-shot, the club is drawn back to about the half-way point of your normal full swing; the force exerted is about half that of the full shot. In your practice swings (and you must have them) it pays to check how much backswing you need before playing the shot.

A good practice drill is to stand with your feet together as you swing. This makes you acutely aware of your balance and stops you from using too much body action and so your rhythm improves noticeably.

Again I stress the importance of smooth acceleration. Do not hold back, do not become fearful of hitting too far and suddenly quit the stroke at the moment of impact.

The key words to keep in mind are 'down' and 'forward'.

On the subject of keeping 'down', there is the constant cry from many pros to their pupils to *keep the head down* irrespective of the shot. Here's how to do it:

1. Hit down.

2. Your knees are bent at the address —keep them bent right through the shot. Straighten your knees, and your body will lift and the head will have no alternative but to also come up. So, keep the knees bent right through.

3. Watch where the ball *was*. In other words, keep your eyes on the back of the ball until *after* it has been struck. The master of this type of concentration is Ben Crenshaw who even goes as far as to concentrate, keeping his eyes stationary, on a single dimple on the ball.

By doing one, two and three, will you master the 'keep down' cry.

HITTING DEAD-CENTRE

One of the finest, most satisfying sounds you will ever hear on a golf course is that sharp C-L-I-C-K of the ball being struck firmly and precisely in the right spot.

And the right spot (in pitching, at least) is the rear underside of the ball, squeezing the blade into that little vee (4) formed by the base of the ball and the ground. That is where you concentrate your mind, focusing down onto the back of the ball, right where you are going to hit it.

4

5

To ensure the right amount of loft, the idea is to take a divot, not the bigger driving divot, but one of about a centimetre or so of turf (5) so that the ball is struck by the dead-centre of the blade. The divot starts directly under the centre of the ball, nowhere else.

The ball is on its way, after that very nice C-L-I-C-K.

Now, let's put it all together, step-by-step, to achieve a well-played pitch.

THE ADDRESS

For these shorter shots, the stance has to be narrowed down. In this sequence (6A–F) I'm playing a three-quarter pitch, so the stance is about three-quarters of the width of the full stance.

It is an open stance with the left foot twisted about a quarter turn towards the target and placed five centimetres from the line. The right foot is square to the line. The ball is centred between the feet and the blade of the club is slightly open.

The left arm and clubshaft are in a straight line, but I'm leaning slightly to the left so that the hands are ahead of the ball.

The knees are flexed and I've had a couple of waggles of the clubhead. That is not a nervous affliction, by the way. The Scots have a saying for it: 'As you waggle so you shall swung'. Not very good grammar, but the message is there. A waggle or two allows you to test your grip pressure and wrist action, but more importantly, stops the tension building up. With a waggle, you are rehearsing what you want to happen.

I'm ready to strike, and not staying stationary for more than a split second, start with two simultaneous movements. A foreward press of the hands and slight kick in with the right knee starts the backswing as a recoil action. The club comes back to the length wanted for distance, but the body weight remains to the left.

The downswing starts with the knees moving forward along the line to the target, and the arms follow, with the pull coming through the left and the right following along to supply the required force.

On impact, the arms take the club through the ball, not the wrists, so that there is no flick; and at the finish of the shot, that 70 per cent of body weight on the left leg has increased to 90–95 per cent. The club finishes about waist-height with the clubface still square to the target, and no rolling of the wrists.

The result? The ball has gone straight or slightly to the right in line with the flag.

6A 6B 6C 6D 6E 6F

I can't emphasise too strongly the importance of pinching the ball against the turf—of getting your clubface down into that vee formed by the ball's underside and the ground.

Stand off from the ball for a few moments to train yourself for the shot coming up. Take two or three swings. Ensure, to your satisfaction, that the low point of the swing is just *at* or *past* the ball, not taking divots but merely skimming the turf. Those swings will set you up for the real shot.

VARIATIONS

By now, you will have gathered that golf is a refreshingly intelligent game in that it demands that you give much thought to what you are about to do.

You will also have noticed that most greens on the majority of courses today are fairly regular. They generally provide fine, well-watered landing places for the pitching shot, especially on the aprons. It follows, therefore, that these are your targets.

Sometimes, that can't be done with the standard pitch played with the ball centred in the address. Sometimes, the wind or the hazards between you and the green require a different pitch shot. You have to think about it. One of the things that champion of past years, Eric Cremin, used to drill into me was: 'Brian, an ounce of thought before a shot is worth a ton afterwards'. True.

THE LOW FLYER

This is played with the ball off the back foot, useful for getting out from under a tree, for example. Some top golfers, though, when in a situation calling for a low flyer, simply play the stroke with a straighter-faced club like the seven-iron. Peter Thomson has always been adept at this particular stroke, mainly because he learned to play it on those wind-swept sandy links courses in Britain.

THE HIGH FLYER

This is a cut-up shot played with the ball off the front foot. You need to have a really good lie for this for you are not hitting down and forward, but sliding the club up and under the ball with the face kept open with left-hand control.

MAKE YOUR PRACTICE WORK

During all this, I expect you have been thinking: 'I must practise my pitches more often'. Of course you should, but what I want you to do is rehearse intelligently. You will get much more satisfaction if you do, and consequently feel better within yourself as well as attain accuracy with these shots.

That great Australian football coach and mover of men, Ron Barassi, has a saying for it. He is constantly drumming into his players at the Melbourne Football Club: 'Practice doesn't make perfect—perfect practice makes perfect!'

To do it successfully, you need to balance a common-sense approach to the job in hand with what will be required in an actual round out on the course. By common-sense, I mean training your mind to judge distance, to choose the type of shot required to meet a given situation and to train your muscles to remember.

Bear in mind, first, the primary points about the pitching stroke itself:

1. The correct open stance with the clubface also slightly opened.
2. The club taken back to the correct height.
3. The swing carried through with smoothness and acceleration, striking the ball down and forwards.
4. No holding back on the shot at the critical moment of impact.
5. The arms taking the club through for the correct amount of follow-through.

Having decided which type of shot you wish to rehearse, and the club required for that shot, the next step is to judge the distance for the shot.

The quickest and simplest way is to set yourself a target. Here (7A) I'm using an umbrella, stuck point first in the ground, but it could be a golf bag or an old shoe box just so long as the target is reasonably conspicuous.

That target is your lobbing point which you have decided is 'X' number of paces short of the flagstick (7B). The aim is to lob the ball on that target so that the ball will run on to the flag (7C).

Ideally, you should start with a distance of about twenty-five to thirty paces from the target, having stepped it out beforehand, fixing the length firmly in your mind. Hit half a dozen balls to the target, then move back five paces and hit another six. Keep moving back on five-pace breaks and all the time retain in your mind the amount of force and acceleration in the shots. By the time you have run out of practice balls you should have worked up to almost a full hit.

Breaks of five paces register on the brain fairly readily; keep your shots within that amount of tolerance and you will seldom miss a green when it comes time to play a round. On most courses, the greens are twenty-eight to thirty paces deep and fifteen to twenty paces wide, so, if you train your mind to judge distances to within five paces and most importantly the lobbing point for a pitching shot, you will soon smarten up your touch. More often than not, your shot will have set you up for a par or even a birdie.

Essentially, with this five-paces method, you are practising with

7A

7B

7C

common-sense and learning how to judge distance and the amount of force and acceleration needed to lob the ball accurately.

CHIPPING

There is ample evidence to show that a good pitch shot player is invariably also a good chip shot player.

Basically, the chip is nothing more than a shortened version of the pitch. The same principles apply to both; the differences come in club selection, shot force and distance.

Pitching is done with the eight-iron through to the sand iron; chipping is done with the five-iron through to the sand iron. Generally, with the chip, you are looking to use a club with less loft so that the little green-side chips are played with the six and seven-irons to run the ball up to the flag. Only in extreme situations would you pull out the heavily lofted club because of the element of risk involved in the shot.

Let me explain. If you chip the ball twenty paces with the six-iron it is a fairly short, quiet shot. But if you hit the ball exactly the same distance from the same spot with the sand iron or wedge, the shot takes 30 to 40 per cent more force. So, if you happen to strike the ball in the belly with the blade then it is going to run 30 to 40 per cent further and perhaps run clean off the green. Do the same with the six and the damage will be far less.

At this stage, it is important to realise that the grip for the chip alters slightly, not so much in essence, but in the position on the shaft.

For the little chips, choke the handle down the shaft near the bottom of the grip (8) progressively letting out more shaft as the shot-distance becomes greater. Choking the handle restricts the leverage which, in turn, tends to make the clubhead a lot lighter and reduce its

8

swinging weight. Or, if you like, you are making the club a toy to hit a toy shot.

Ball placements, stance and address are generally the same as for the pitch.

In the chip, the head must be set slightly ahead of the ball. A good way to check if your stance is correct is to hold the top of the club between thumb and forefinger under the chin. The line of the club is just in front of the ball, and that then will be the lowest part of the swing arc (9).

9

Now (10A) you are ready to play the chip, recalling the essentials of the pitch shot. Obviously, the backswing is even less than for the pitch and there is only a small amount of hand and wrist action in taking the club back for that limited length (10B).

Hit down and forward, brushing or bruising the turf at or past the ball, keeping the left arm and shaft in a straight line as you swing through (10C, D). The essential thing is to have the left arm lead the stroke which, from what I've seen, is the exact opposite to what many golfers do. Their cardinal sin is to flick the wrist at the moment of impact with the clubhead passing in front of the left arm. It is certainly no way to be accurate with the chip shot.

TAKING WEIGHT

When it comes to chipping and those little pitch-and-run shots, Peter Thomson was top-class in those years of his string of British Open victories and he still is, for that matter, on the Seniors' circuit in America.

Those short shots epitomise Peter's whole approach to golf. His view is that golf is truly *the* thinking game, calling for calmness and logical observation. His credo is: sum up your situation, decide what type of shot should be played, then give it your best. He has rightly observed that around-the-greens play demands judgement above all else. It seems an obvious thing, I know, but it is amazing how many people fall for the trap of thinking that 'giving it your best shot' actually means 'giving it a whack'.

One way to develop your touch for distance for these short shots is to throw the ball underarm a few times when you have the opportunity. Don't hurl it, but deliver it towards the flag delicately and with the correct weight. 'Weight' is a term you will hear used in lawn bowls constantly, and we can apply it here to golf. All the word

10A

10B

10C

10D

really means is judging the correct amount of momentum to get the bowl across the green to the little white ball, called the 'jack'.

It is worth watching a good lawn bowler like our World Championship silver medallist, John Snell, who, incidentally, is also a dab hand with a set of golf clubs. When John bowls, there is a little bit of wrist-arching as his hand reaches the end of the back-swing, but the bowl is delivered with the arm. It's the same with those pitch and chip shots. John doesn't deliver the bowl with a flick of the wrist at the moment of release to send the bowl *up*—you shouldn't hit your golf shots like that, either. The clubface will give the ball the loft it needs.

Try it for yourself. Crouch down and deliver the golf ball towards the flag (11). It's the best way I know to develop and train yourself to judge the 'weight' of a chip from the edge of the green. More importantly, perhaps, is the feeling you will get that this part of golf, especially, is not an *up* game, but a *down* and *forwards* game.

With chipping, this rear view (12) might give you a better appreciation of the feeling I'm talking about. It also shows the relationship of the head to the ball and the body's position at this stage of the stroke.

11

12

A Fine Finish

EIGHTEENTH, ROYAL MELBOURNE COMPOSITE

Everyone knows Royal Melbourne — or do they?

The Royal is seen on television more often than any other of our Australian courses. Each November it plays host to the Australian PGA Championship, covered for more than 200 television relay points and stations throughout the nation by the ABC. But how many people realise that Royal Melbourne is not one, but three courses?

For fifty-one weeks of the year, members and visitors can choose to play either the eighteen holes of the west course or eighteen on the east course. For that other week, each November, competitors in the PGA event play a composite layout made up of holes from both east and west courses.

Whichever layout, I've heard Royal Melbourne described as brutal, and demanding the utmost control over both strokes and nerves. I must admit it to be an awesome place with fast greens and cavernous bunkers.

Yet, some years ago, *Australian Golf* magazine ran a poll among leading Australian players to determine the nation's greatest course. Their choice? Royal Melbourne, naturally. I say 'naturally', for despite its awesomeness and the demands it places on those who play there, one cannot but be aware of the feelings the Royal provokes and inspires.

Ben Crenshaw said it best. After years of reading about Royal Melbourne, but never having the opportunity to play there, he strolled onto the course late one evening and declared it, '. . . as beautiful as they wrote in the books only more so'.

So, now we are about to play one of the finest, if not *the* finest, finishing holes in the country, as Mr Average should play it! It is the Eighteenth for both the east and the composite layouts, where every PGA champion finishes his round. The Eighteenth is one of the best examples I know of the need to play deadly accurate pitch shots.

Before we start, it may be of some comfort to learn that in 1978, of the qualifiers for the final thirty-six holes of that year's championship, only two played the Eighteenth under par! Fifty-two made it in regulation figures and forty-six were over par. The average score for the hole was 4·58.

Off the tee and ahead of you is the 395-metre long fairway, slightly dog-leg left. It pays to aim slightly right to avoid the copse of trees on fairway left and to give you a better line into the green. 'Better' is only a relative word here perhaps, for in front of the green are those famous Royal Melbourne bunkers built the old-fashioned way, with horse and scoop. The approach to take from this lie is to hit a five-iron to lay up short of the traps, then pitch in with a wedge over the sand.

The result leaves a six-metre putt slightly uphill. (Incidentally, in this photograph, as with all in this book, the flagstick has been left in the cup to provide you with a clearer reference for each putt.)

Down in two at Royal Melbourne's Eighteenth for a one-over five. Not too ambitious, but as those figures show we're in good company on this hole. It also emphasises the theory that you should always play your own game. Always be realistic and if a par four on a hole like this is really a par five for you, then aim for that. Forget what it says on the scorecard and play to make that par five your personal best or, if you like, your own true par.

A Nice One to Birdie

TENTH, METROPOLITAN GC, MELBOURNE—PAR FOUR, 427 METRES

These days, the Victorian Open Championship is more than just another State title. The event always attracts the top players, professional and amateur, and as a result has won for itself a rather special place on the Australian golfing calendar.

One of the things that makes the tournament one to watch is the presence of the nation's top women amateurs, playing in a teams event. In 1983 there was an added attraction in the form of a head-to-head clash between Jane Lock and Jan Stephenson. Jane won the contest, which did not surprise the wiseheads—they remembered that it was Jane who set the ladies' record on Metropolitan in 1981 with a fine 66. On Metropolitan, one of Melbourne's best sandbelt courses, that is not an easy record to achieve.

After the outward nine, the run home starts with this long par four. It looks easy, but is not. For the club player, he is best served by looking at the Tenth as a five. For the pros, it is a nice one to par or, better still, birdie.

Yet, the pros can find it a struggle, too. When the 1979 Australian Open was played over Metropolitan, the Tenth averaged 4·61 strokes on the final two days. Only two players birdied here, while pars and bogies were equal on 54.

The tee shot has to be particularly well-placed, but unless you are capable of booming a 300-metre drive, the lake at the dog-leg doesn't come into play.

The Second, around the corner, also demands a long shot preferably with some draw.

Beware of the traps—curator Bill Podesta likes his bunker walls to be hard and steep. So, it is better to lay up a little short. The clubman will be doing that anyway, although probably not from choice.

From anywhere near eighty paces out, the pitch has to be dead-accurate over the sand, yet once on the green, the beautifully manicured surface is perfect for getting down in two.

For Openers

FIRST, VICTORIA GC, MELBOURNE—PAR FOUR, 233 METRES

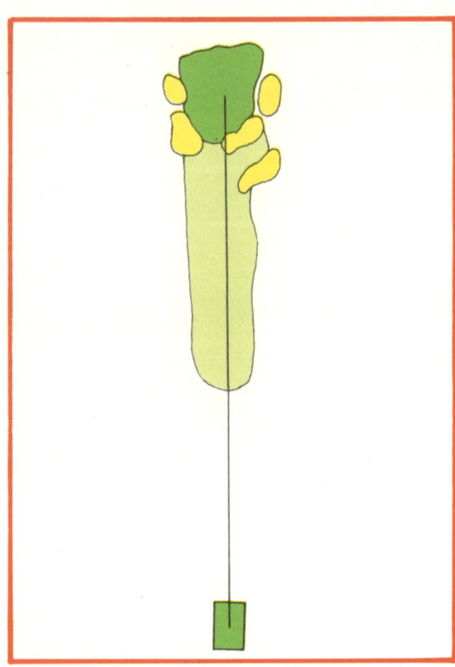

If the club golfer is to collect a par anywhere at all on Victoria's layout, then this is the place to do it!

The First is a delightful hole, straight down from the clubhouse, alongside the sweeping driveway and into the corner formed by Park Road, Cheltenham. A full-blooded drive off the tee has been known to frighten the motorists on more than one occasion. But, that is not the game plan.

From the tee, the heart of the First is obvious—an elevated green surrounded by very deep sandtraps, and the target choice for the ambitious is green-centre.

Remember, though, that the aim is to procure par and the conservative golfer will strive for a straight long iron to lay up short of the green. That well-struck drive then leaves nothing by a short wedge up and onto the rolling green and in all probability, two mere putts.

The pros treat the First as a great birdie possibility. The average golfer should look at the same hole as a par possibility, with a better-than-even chance of getting it! The secret is accuracy off the tee.

If nothing else, Victoria's First proves the theory of thinking out a plan of attack—and not necessarily the obvious one—and then sticking to it.

Through the Pines

EIGHTH, ROYAL ADELAIDE GC—
PAR FOUR, 341 METRES

This picturesque hole offers some relief after some of the earlier fours on Royal Adelaide's marram and sand dunes. Basically, it calls for a drive and a short iron and as such is a good test of your short game.

The tee is long and narrow and slightly elevated. It is, however, lined by Royal Adelaide's famous pine trees and can be penal for both hookers and slicers.

Aiming point off the tee should be a small stand of pines left-hand rear of the green to set up the best line to the flag. Once clear of the pines around the tee, second shots provide an opportunity for well-struck pitches. The ordinary golfer will be looking at a shot of between 100 and 140 paces. From the normal tees, the cleverly sited mounds on the right side catch many shots.

With a tailwind, the choice should be a wedge to get the ball up high and obtain carry to the slightly sloping green. Better to aim for the front for an upslope putt.

The Eighth is the type of 'easy' par four that is called a sleeper—I say 'easy' because slight carelessness can result readily in a five or six.

A straight drive is needed at the Eighth at Royal Adelaide, as the majestic rows of pines will punish anything off-line.

4 Beating the Bunker

There is no doubt that one of the more important clubs in the bag is the sand iron. A marvellously-designed instrument, the club will repay its cost many times over for those little shots around the green besides the ones in the traps.

One of the first of the modern golfers to use a sand iron was Gene Sarazen. Niblicks in all shapes and sizes had been used since the nineteenth century until Gene Sarazen unveiled an iron made specifically with a big flange to get the ball up and out of the sand. It used to be said of Sarazen that he would sometimes aim at the bunker just to show how good he was at getting out of it!

The biggest problem most people have with trap shots is their fear of them. The ball lobs in the bunker and the closer they get to actually having to play the shot, the more their confidence just runs away. They regard sand as their enemy when, with a little knowledge, it can become their friend. If that is your problem, then look at it this way:

Normally, with a sand shot, there is no contact between club and ball. If the shot is played correctly, the ball simply rises out of its lie on a cushion of sand. Thus, your margin for error is far greater than with other shots, so why not make the most of it.

The secret in hitting a good trap shot is to let the sand iron do its job.

To do that, some knowledge of the way in which the club works will not only be useful, it might also help overcome a fear of sand play.

Turn the club over and look at the flange on the bottom. It's called the 'bounce' and that is exactly what it does—allowing the clubface to skid through the sand at the proper depth and lift the ball out on a cushion of the stuff (1).

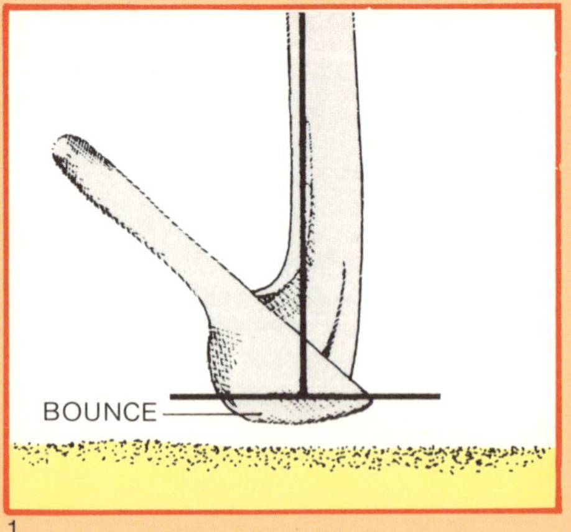

1

The bounce is quite broad with the trailing edge set distinctly lower than the leading edge which is why the club doesn't bury. That trailing edge, in effect, works as a rudder, enabling the club to slice through the sand and allowing you to undercut the ball.

Obviously, sand irons come in many forms and it pays to check with your pro to see if yours is right for the kind of sand used in the bunkers on your course.

For example, if those bunkers contain soft, fluffy sand like that at the Australian Club in Sydney, where the National Open was played in 1982, then you will need a sand iron with a very broad bounce. On the other hand, most Melbourne bunkers have a type of hard sand, requiring an iron with a very shallow flange so that the club has only a slight skidding effect. If you strike extremely hard, well-packed sand, and that doesn't happen too often, it sometimes pays to use your pitching wedge, which has only a flange parallel to the bottom of the blade.

Always remember that for the trailing edge to do its job for you, the clubface must be set open at the address. It's made to be used that way. Also remember, however, that the rules of golf do not allow you to ground the club in the sand before the shot is taken.

Now, let us look at the techniques required for using the sand iron and, with them, some of the secrets of good trap play.

GRIP AND PRESSURE

This is a singularly different shot to all the others in the book, with the exception of the flip shot, which we shall come to in a later chapter.

The difference lies in the fact that the wrists are hinged to allow the clubhead to pass the left arm as it comes through. So, the wrists must be reasonably loose as must be the grip pressure—just enough to keep the fingers closed. The primary pressure points are on the last three fingers of the left hand.

The grip itself is the one used for a deliberately sliced shot. Far from merely taking a normal grip and twisting the face open, here's how to do it:

1. Hold the clubface straight, but have the vees formed by the forefinger and thumb of each hand pointing towards the left shoulder.
2. Now, let the hands come back to the normal position and the clubface will twist open to the point where the 'bounce' will be able to do its work through the sand (2).

2

ENTRY POINTS

Most people know that in a trap shot the sand is struck behind the ball. What is not so well known is that the entry point in the sand for the clubhead shifts according to the nature of the sand.

The way to determine the sand type is with the feet since the rules prevent you from using the obvious method, with the club. There can be no practice swings in a bunker.

Test the sand the way the pros do by wriggling and scuffling with your feet. For example, if it's very hard and you have trouble scratching your studs in, then you are going to have to hit very close to the ball. The looser the sand the further back the strike point.

3

4

In the photograph (3) the line drawn in the sand indicates where to hit for each type or texture—firm, average and soft, represented by the three balls.

Hard sand: Your entry point is two to three centimetres behind the ball.

Average sand: (Similar to the type I'm playing from at Royal Melbourne.) Your entry point is five to six centimetres behind the ball.

Soft, fluffy sand: The entry point is ten to twelve centimetres back.

In the address, the entry point should always be at a spot opposite the centre between your feet. The reason is that you are conditioned to playing your pitching wedge and chip shots from this position.

The ball is always ahead of centre (and thus, the entry point) according to the texture of the sand. The next photograph shows the club striking the sand on the line determined by its type (4).

As with all shots, there has to be a focus point for the eyes. In the trap, it is the point of entry.

I've known many golfers who prefer to look directly at the ball. But, in teaching, I've found the method of looking at the entry point in the sand to be not only more logical, but also more successful. It does, however, take some practice to focus down on nothing but sand.

Not all clubs, unfortunately, have practice traps, but go down to the beach sometime and experiment on the sand there with your swing. I would advise against taking a ball with you. Draw a line on the beach and straddle it with your feet; grip the club loosely and just practise making a three-quarter swing, striking at the line, letting the flange skid through the sand and complete the stroke with the same amount of follow-through as you had in the backswing.

The beach method gives you the feeling or the knack of letting the sole of the club bounce through the sand. At the same time, you will be concentrating your ability to focus on a patch of sand and to hit it.

If your club has a practice trap, make use of it as regularly as you can. Naturally, there's nothing like the real thing (5A–F).

This is the standard trap shot for green-side bunkers. Normally, you would be aiming to carry the ball ten to fifteen paces, but for anything less, you restrict your swing slightly; anything more, say up to twenty paces, you increase your swing length.

In both cases, although you may be shortening or lengthening your swing, you always hit behind the ball, the distance being determined by the sand texture.

BEHIND THE SWING

Earlier, I talked of the 'cartwheel effect' in the golf swing; how each stroke represents either the full arc or part of it, depending on the amount of force to be taken for the distance involved in the shot. Where the trap-shot swing differs is in its shape.

Again, it is because of those loose, hinged wrists and the looser grip required for the shot.

Together, the wrists and the grip produce more of a U-shaped swing where the club is picked up at each end, making the arc nowhere near as wide as it would be for a normal shot off turf.

The trouble with many golfers' sand shots is that they try to scoop up the ball, especially if faced with a high bunker wall between them and the green. It's a psychological thing, I suppose, but what usually happens is that they set their body weight on the right (or incorrect) leg and try to flick the ball up. As a result, the clubhead strikes too far back and is actually leaving the sand as it nears the ball.

The secret is to control the lowest point of the swing.

You are unlikely to scoop if you keep your knees bent but relaxed at the address and right throughout the stroke. Doing this helps to keep your

5A

5B

5C

5D

5E

5F

body down and to resist the urge to hit the ball up.

Body weight is set towards the left side; not too much, just enough to know that you are leaning left of centre. The arms are hanging, as if they are leather straps off your shoulders. The left arm and clubshaft do not form a straight line at the address; there's a slight kink between the left arm and shaft, with the hands above rather than in front of the ball. This increases the loft and further promotes that skidding effect of the flange at the bottom of the club.

In the takeaway the wrists break quickly, while the knees remain flexed (6A). The backswing is a reasonably slow one, (6B) and at the top (6C) there is a fairly full wrist action, readying them to provide the sharp acceleration into the stroke as the knees move left towards the target (6D).

On entering the impact area the wrists start to unwind, but the body (because of those relaxed knees) remains down.

Probably the most salient point here is to see that the clubhead passes under the left arm; the left wrist hinges noticeably, letting the right hand pass underneath the left wrist. With that movement, the clubhead will achieve its bumping, skidding effect through the sand (6E). In short, the wrists hinge at the bottom of the arc, the key moment of control.

At the end of the stroke the body weight has moved fluently through even more to the left side, while the follow-through equals the amount of backswing taken at the start of the stroke. The ball has risen on its cushion of sand on its way to the target, the flagstick (6F).

THE LONGER TRAP SHOT

The next time you watch one of the championship tour events on television take note of how the leading

6A

6D

6B

6E

6C

6F

pros tackle the sand. You can learn much, especially from the slow-motion replays.

Immediately apparent is the fact that the players who take their time and swing easily and smoothly are the ones who consistently get out of the traps with accuracy.

Certainly, stars like Greg Norman or Graham Marsh occasionally will duff a sand shot but you will notice that it is always a long time before they duff another. Usually, as soon as the round ends, they will head for the practice traps to work out any problem they caught out on the course.

Invariably, they will never rush a trap shot, but spend several moments working out their angles and best approach before taking their address. When they do strike it is always with fluency and acceleration, giving the ball plenty of sand to act as a cushion. It is usually very spectacular, bringing plenty of applause from the crowd.

When it comes to the longer trap shots of between twenty to forty paces, the differences in the techniques used, against those for the green-side sand play, are quite marked. It can be an awkward shot but played correctly can give you enormous confidence in your overall bunker play.

Oddly enough, the longer trap shot is similar to a duffed pitch shot played off turf. Imagine, if you will, duffing a pitch intended to go about seventy paces by hitting the ground about three centimetres behind the ball. Instead of the intended length, the ball travels only about thirty paces. Well, that's your longer trap shot.

At the address (7) take your

8A

8B

8D

8E

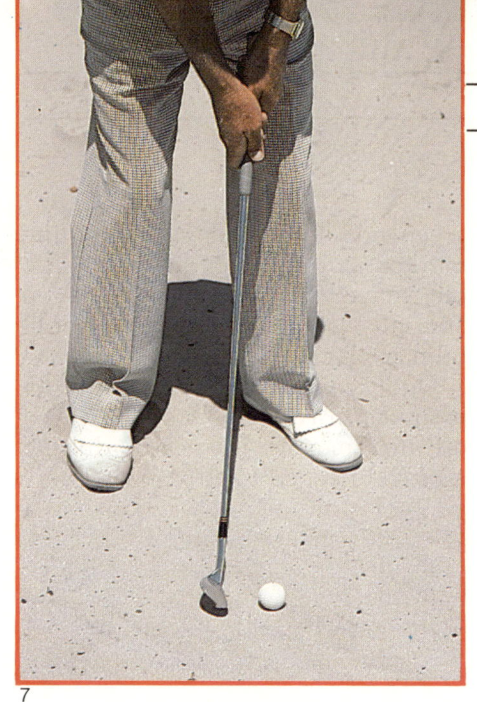
7

standard grip as you would for a normal shot played off turf. The vees formed by the forefingers and thumbs are pointing towards your right eye, the left wrist and arm are quite firm. The ball is opposite the midway point between your feet, and 70 per cent of the body weight is on the left leg.

Importantly, the clubface is square so as to help you to aim the shot better, and your eyes are focused on the entry point in the sand about three centimetres behind the ball (8A).

Although the shot is slightly stronger than the one used for green-side trap play, you still keep those knees bent right through the shot (8B, C). The body thus stays down, and moves smoothly with the shot to the left towards the target (8D).

At this point it becomes obvious how much the shot varies from the shorter trap stroke (8E). The club hasn't passed the left arm, since the wrists are not hinged. In fact, that firm left wrist and arm are leading through the stroke, which is a drive forward with a low follow-through (8F).

Whether the trap shot is short or long, always move your knees through the shot, transferring your body weight towards the target.

8C

8F

BURIED BALL

Every golfer is inclined to disappointment when he gets a bad lie—it's only human. Whether or not you allow that feeling to weigh on the mind and influence your next shot determines what type of golfer you really are.

More shots are missed (and added to your score!) through lack of concentration and control than through any other fault. When you get a bad break, look upon the recovery as a challenge and get on with the job. Knowing the technique for recovery cuts the load in half.

In trap play, one of the most seemingly daunting tasks for the average player is recovering from a lie where the ball is buried in the sand. The immediate temptation is to blast at the ball with the club, the stroke being generated more by temper than anything else. Don't do it.

While the technique for salvaging a buried ball is straightforward enough, the real secret lies in not trying to be ambitious. Be content just to hit the green even if the ball stops a long way from the cup. You will always hole more long putts than you ever will with sand shots.

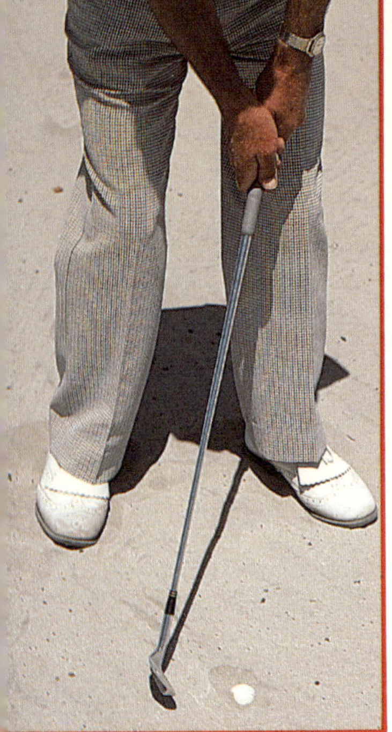
9A

9B

9C

9D

DEEPLY-BURIED BALL

If the ball is buried straight down (9A) this indicates that the sand is quite soft and you will take a point of entry about six to seven centimetres behind the ball.

Set the ball back a little in the stance and take the grip with more strength than you would for the normal green-side trap shot (9B).

The clubface should be closed, the vees of the forefingers and thumbs pointing away to the right of your nose. The aiming point for the shot is slightly to the outside of a direct line to the target (9C).

The shot itself is really a very heavy chop or stabbing one with the club picked up sharply in the backswing (9D). Drive the clubhead deeply into the sand, making the ball pop up (9E–G). Follow-through is minimal with this kind of stabbing action (9H) and the clubhead will not be going through over the left arm.

Don't try to finesse the shot, for the ball, popping up, will run on more than your normal bunker stroke.

PARTLY-BURIED BALL

A variation on the theme is effective when the ball is not completely buried. Play the same technique but keep the clubface slightly open rather than closed, hitting down with that same chopping action about seven centimetres behind the ball.

UP THE FACE

By far the most crucial factor in golf is your mental make-up. I keep stressing this point because I know and understand through hard experience just how much fear of a shot can produce mistakes.

An awkward lie only adds to the tightness inside one. Stay calm and make logical observations of your situation.

A good example in bunker play is when the ball is on an upslope in the trap. If the slope is one of more than 45 degrees, you will approach the shot in one way; anything less than this, and the shot will be played differently.

10A

10B

9E

9F

9G

9H

First, a lie on a sharp incline. Like the longer trap shot, the technique is that of the duffed pitch or chip shot.

At the address square off as *if* to hit the ball cleanly, centred with the front foot higher than the ball, the back foot below it (10A). Keep the clubface square and lean onto the left leg, bringing the body vertical to the slope.

As I said, take the address as *if* to hit the ball cleanly, but in fact you hit into the sand a fraction behind it (10B) driving the clubhead into the bunker wall itself (10C).

There is no follow-through to speak of (10D) and the ball will pop fairly smartly, so don't go looking for a high degree of accuracy with this shot.

If the lie is on a gentle upslope, set yourself at a right angle to the slope. In other words, you are not leaning forwards this time, the body weight being more on the right leg.

With the swing, you actually try to follow the angle of the slope, still taking sand with an entry point about seven to eight centimetres behind the ball.

10C

10D

DOWN THE FACE

What I've said about digesting the facts of your situation in the bunker applies even more so when the lie is on the backslope.

If the incline is one of more than 35 to 40 degrees, then the shot usually is not on and you will be better off looking for another way, perhaps hitting sideways out of the trap. In this situation, a good pro will eliminate the risk and go for a safety shot every time.

Even on a more gentle downslope, the ball most times will come out low and hot so it is a dangerous shot at best.

But, if after weighing up the facts, you believe the shot is on, here is how to tackle it:

Address the ball exactly as you would for a normal green-side trap shot, then lean forwards so that your body is at right angles to the slope

(11A). In other words, the body weight is more on the left leg. The clubface is kept well and truly open and the knees are bent, but relaxed to keep the body down.

In actual fact, it is as if you are playing off a flat lie, but the whole picture has been tilted. By leaning on your front leg, you are able to pick up the club more abruptly, making the backswing almost vertical (11B).

Again, the impact area behind the ball is relative to the sand's texture and with the clubface open, the 'bounce' will skid through, lifting sand and ball (11C).

This photograph (11D) illustrates perfectly the need to keep those eyes down a fraction of a second longer after the ball has been struck. The follow-through for this downslope shot is as you would play your normal trap shot (11E).

11A

11B

GAINING HEIGHT

Telecasts of the Australian PGA Championship from Royal Melbourne make this a well-known bunker.

Distinctive because of its sod wall, the trap guards the right-hand approach to the Seventh on Royal Melbourne's championship layout. Its depth and the green elevation force the player landing there from the tee to get more height into his shot than he would normally.

How the pros play it—how you should play this type of trap shot (12A–F)—is to use the standard technique for green-side bunkers, only more so.

In other words, the stance and swing line is well to the left of the flag, probably about eight to ten paces, and the clubface is twisted open very severely, targetting eight to ten paces to the *right* of the stick.

As with the normal trap shot, the knees are bent, bringing the body right down, the wrists break fairly sharply as the club comes back and the clubface is brought down into the sand very hard, the point of entry here being about six centimetres behind the ball.

By twisting the clubface open as severely as suggested, you are adding considerably to the loft of the blade.

Literally belt down into the sand; with that flange bumping through,

12A

12D

11C

11D

11E

the ball tends to climb a lot higher.

It can be a dangerous shot, but at this hole, the hard part really comes next . . . putting over the Seventh's undulations and slopes. From the 1981 PGA tournament, I have a mental picture of the look of amazement that came over Seve Ballesteros' face when his approach putt took five paces of borrow, missed the cup and kept on rolling for another eight or nine. Seve went on to win the title, of course, but like many others before and since, he discovered that Royal Melbourne's Seventh is definitely not an easy hole.

12B

12C

12E

12F

MORE ON SAND

A final thought on the subject of sand . . . The elements of trap play are easily defined; it is the conditions you will find in various types of bunkers which provide the challenge.

So, you have to think about those conditions before playing any shot out of sand and decide on the technique most suited to meet them.

One of the factors highlighted by trap play techniques is the benefit to be gained from swinging parallel to your stance. Consider for a moment how a trap shot is played . . .

The stance is open with the feet aiming left of the target, but the clubface is pointed to the right. With the club swung parallel to your stance, the ball will neither follow the stance-line nor the line from the clubface. It will split the difference and head for the flag.

It is virtually a controlled slice. The club is *not* pushed away outside the body then pulled back across, but it is swung *parallel* to the body. The action increases the skidding motion through the sand for which this type of iron was designed, at the same time as increasing the loft of the ball.

It doesn't matter whether you have deliberately opened or hooded the blade or have it square, in all shots with driver and iron, swing parallel to the body.

In giving lessons, I try to get people to retain this thought for most shots they play between tee and green. Once they get the concept, they feel they don't have to change their swing very much to play all types of shots. It's a short-cut to lower scores all round the course.

Wind and Sand

SEVENTH, METROPOLITAN GC,
MELBOURNE—PAR THREE, 210 METRES

It sounds simple, doesn't it? A little ol' par three of just over 200 metres . . . but! When Metropolitan Golf Club in Melbourne looked at a re-building programme years ago, the

Seventh was one hole they decided to leave untouched. Probably they reckoned on it being dangerous enough as it was! At least, this patch of Metropolitan is fair to everybody, hacker and hotshot alike.

On the card, the Seventh is a one-shotter to the green, then down in two for a par.

However, anyone who walks away with a three on his card has to have a smile on his face. Wind from anywhere west of north can make the Seventh an almost certain bogey hole and I've seen a few likely-looking Victorian Open winners leave the green shaking their heads.

When the Australian Open was played at Metropolitan in 1979, the Seventh was rated the second hardest hole on the course. Out of the 120 rounds on the final two days, the Seventh produced 66 pars, 47 bogeys and three double-bogeys, for an average score on the hole of 3·41. There were only four birdies.

The real trouble at the Seventh is concentrated in and around the green, which is not over-large and is well-protected by deep traps. It is the type of hole where the average club-player must be very aware of his limitations and play accordingly.

On this day the following breeze is sounding a siren's song and it seems a great opportunity to go for green-centre with a four-wood.

At the last moment, that deceptive breeze has gusted and caught the

ball, sweeping it into the sand guarding the left front of the green. At least the lie is a straightforward one and gives the opportunity to try out the technique we've been discussing for the longer trap shot. The danger here is skulling the ball over the back of the green, so I drop it a little shorter than I would normally like, leaving me twenty paces of putting to get it down in two.

Still, one over on Metropolitan's Seventh puts me in very good company and any club-player who does the same can count his blessings.

Wind and sand combine to make Metropolitan's Seventh a test for any aspiring trap player.

A Little Something on the Side

ELEVENTH, THE LAKES GC, SYDNEY—
PAR FIVE, 505 METRES

There is nothing deceptive about the Eleventh at the Lakes. It looks hard and is hard—a beautiful test of golf.

Not the least of the problems here is the one created by the water, all the way along the starboard side of the fairway to within spitting distance of the green. And just to add to the dubious pleasure of all this is the fact that as the Eleventh dog-legs right, there is always a left-to-right slope, making every lie below foot level for the right-hander. That is bound to encourage slicing which usually means a watery grave. And since distances over water are deceptive, it is so tempting after a big drive to get home in two.

David Graham knows about that. In 1981, twice he tried to carry the water. Twice he was unsuccessful, eventually opting for the safer, but longer way home around dry land.

The criterion for securing par at the Eleventh is to use the tee shot to set up for the second, aiming well left of the fairway.

From here a well-struck wood will still only take you to six or seven-iron distance from the green and that has to be struck well enough to carry both lake and front green-side trap. With the iron, aim for green centre, and if you must err, be so on the long side rather than the short.

The traps around the green are fairly straightforward requiring only the technique and expertise you have learned in drills and practice.

Down Dale, Up Hill

TENTH, VICTORIA GC, MELBOURNE—
PAR FOUR, 348 METRES

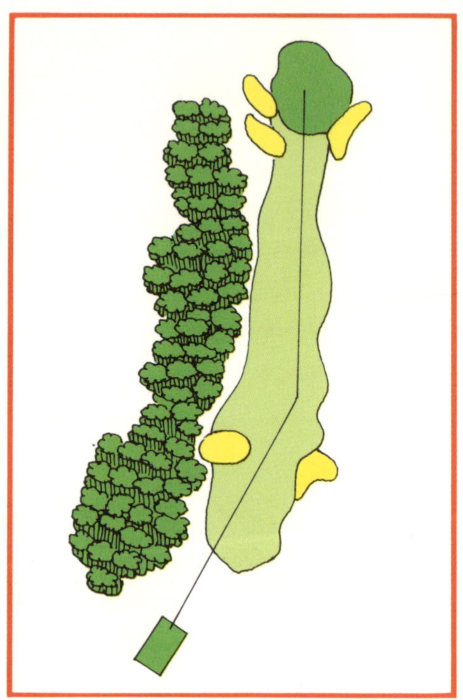

Take a look at the card and the Tenth seems to be a relatively easy par four. That view can alter swiftly from the tee!

The fairway runs down the natural slope away from the tee, dog-legs to the left and heads up again to the green, which, naturally, is well-bunkered.

And the fairway bunker 110 metres in front of the tee is not there to add beauty to the hole. Any drive topped off the tee inevitably rolls straight into the sand, and that means a virtual penalty before the golfer gets anywhere near the green.

The aim off the tee is towards the right-hand side of the fairway to allow an open shot, probably with a three-iron, for the second or approach shot. Again, keep right to avoid the green-side traps. That leaves a smallish chip up from the front of the green and a couple of putts for a one-over score.

No, the Tenth at Victoria is not a hole to be taken lightly.

One of the seven bunkers that surround the Seventh Green at Metropolitan.

From Tee to Green

You can't become Number One without determination, patience, concentration and the correct mental attitude.

Take, for example, the American Tom Watson. Among his many tournament successes have been the British and US Opens. When asked why, Watson pinpointed the reasons for his achievements to the fact that he makes a 100 per cent effort every time he addresses the ball; that he always tries to play within himself; and that he is blessed with an ability to learn from his successes, as well as his failures.

One of the key factors in Watson's ability off the tee is the tempo of his swing.

Yet, there too he has worries. Under pressure, his swing gets too fast and he has to slow it down consciously to maintain tempo, relying on muscle memory to overcome the problem.

Muscle memory. No one can achieve that state in their game without the training which comes from practising drills and routines. It begins with the realisation that one's muscles are almost certainly not trained properly for the golf swing. The next step is to learn to do naturally what has been unnatural.

In 1929 Bobby Jones talked about what he called 'the mental hazards of golf'. He said: 'The golf swing is a most complicated combination of muscular actions, too complex to be controlled by objective conscious mental effort. Consequently, we must rely a good deal upon the instinctive reactions acquired by long practice. It has been my experience that the more completely we depend upon this instinct, the more thoroughly we can divest the subjective mind of conscious control and the more perfectly we can execute our shot'.

STROKE DYNAMICS

At this stage, it is worth making the point again that golf is a simple sport, made harder only by the people who play it.

Stripped of all its mysteries, theories, dogmas and conundrums, golf is essentially a game where you hit a ball to a target. Swinging the club to achieve that aim is basically the same movement as throwing a stone. You think least of how to do it, most of all about hitting that target.

You set, turn and throw (1A–D). Remember?

Those are the primary points about the golf swing, but to do that the seventy, eighty, ninety or more times it takes you to get around the course, a person needs to train the muscles and the thought patterns.

The best pre-practice or pre-round exercise I have found is a simple, yet effective one which will take only a few minutes. It stretches the back, arm, leg and shoulder muscles, pushing them into a state of suppleness.

First of all (and it does not matter which club you use) place a club

1A

1B

1C

1D

behind the back with the shaft through the crooked elbows (2A). Set your feet in the golf stance, bow from the waist but keep the back straight and just slightly flex the knees. You should be poised and balanced as if you are about to dive into a swimming pool.

To make the exercise a positive one, place a ball between your feet in the centre or preferably, use a mirror in this position. The movement you are about to make is a pivot around that central point and, as the golf swing demands a focal point for the eyes, a mirror enables you to do this most effectively.

Do not worry too much about your feet and legs at this stage, but from that stance, watching the ball or mirror carefully, pivot the trunk to the top of the full backswing (2B). The head has remained still, the left shoulder is under the chin and there is only a faint shifting of weight to the right side.

Do a few of these pivots to get used to the feeling of coiling the body into this simulation of the backswing.

Next, concentrate on the hips and knees. The left knee should be going across about half-way and the left heel rising slightly, about two to three centimetres. Anymore is too much. This is a 45-degree turn across hips and knees and at the same time, you are turning that left shoulder under the chin in a 90-degree coil.

Now, starting from stance-centre, do the full turn. First, pivot to the right for the backswing, then the opposite way for the follow-through. In this latter movement, the right knee is coming in to touch the left, the weight shifts all the way across to be balanced on the left leg and the right shoe is on its point at the conclusion of the pivot (2C). So:

1. Concentrate on a steady head with the left shoulder getting up under the chin.

2. Do the 45 degrees of hip and knee turn from left to right.

3. The full turn for the follow-through.

The exercise not only teaches you the feeling for the complete swing but, at the same time, loosens up and relaxes the muscles, training them for the job ahead.

2A

2B

2C

3A

3B

3C

Looked at from another angle, the bow from the waist can be seen more clearly (3A–C). The body is maintained at a constant tilt right through the movement, head and back being set forward about thirty centimetres.

In the first, the left shoulder is more apparent in its backswing position as being lower than the right and then the reverse in the follow-through. In turning through this movement, there is no strain on the back because hips and shoulders are all in a line.

Now, I know that goes against a commonly-held belief that people with bad backs should keep their bodies stationary when they swing a golf club. They are under the misapprehension that by keeping the body still and swinging with the arms, they will not strain their backs.

However, this method actually produces more body twist than does the correct movement.

In fact, they should make an equal type of pivot where the left knee comes right across in the backswing, the hips turning by the same amount as the shoulders, then the same in the follow-through.

And those people with bad backs should take comfort in the fact that, in golf, many of the top pros are sufferers too. Ballesteros, Trevino and Marsh have all suffered at one time or another from various forms of back ailments. Sometimes, as in Trevino's case, it can mean an operation, but mostly they exercise as a daily ritual for either prevention or relief.

But, you will never see them swinging from the arms and shoulders and not turning the hips and legs.

BEFORE YOU HIT

The starting point for any well-executed stroke is the placement of the ball. I cannot stress enough the importance of taking your stance with the ball in the correct position for the club you have selected.

Over the years, there has been confusion over this, caused chiefly, I believe, by the preference of many leading professionals for playing almost every shot with the ball in line with the left heel.

Ben Hogan was the first world-class player to do so and recommend that all shots be played with the ball in the same position. His belief was that it was the stance which had to be adjusted. Since Hogan, many others on the world circuits have chosen to do the same.

Many beginners seeing and reading about this method believe that this is what they have to do. What is often overlooked is that players of average calibre do not have the leg and wrist actions to play that way successfully. They have not trained and practised for years as the top players have done.

What may suit Ben Hogan, or Jack Nicklaus or anybody else, for that matter, may not be best for you.

I prefer both the beginner and the average player to take their stance with the ball in the best position for the variety of strokes and clubs they have to play. In the light of modern tournament play, this may sound conservative, even old-fashioned, but it is worth remembering that the Hogans of the world started out in this way and changed their techniques only after much experimentation.

Starting with the wedge and the ball in the centre between the feet, the positions move forward as the clubs become straighter in the face until the last ball in the line is teed up for driving off the left heel (4).

Primarily, there are three areas of ball placement. They enable you, first with the short and middle irons, to hit down into the ball, pinching it against the turf; then with the long irons and fairway woods to brush the turf and finally, to hit a slightly rising blow with the driver with the ball in line with the left heel.

At the same time, there is only one true place to collect the ball—in the middle of the clubface. Where the

4

variation comes into the different strokes is in the impact points on the ball. They vary with the club used.

To illustrate the difference, the first photograph (5A) shows that the ball is clearly struck by the short iron on the underside, skidding up the face to create backspin as it flies.

The driver, however, because its stroke is a rising one should collect the ball in its centre (5B). You will notice that the clubhead is a centimetre lower than the base of the ball, demanding you to strike in this way.

Because of that deeper face on the driver, a correctly-struck tee shot should just clip the top of the tee-peg. The impact point is on the back of the ball and not the underside, as with the wedge or nine-iron.

The practice routine shown (6A, B) is one which you can do in the backyard to produce the 'feel' for correct tee-height in the swing and show whether you are toeing or heeling the ball.

Place a tee-peg in the ground at about full height, sole the clubface on the grass and set a second peg about two centimetres wider than the clubhead. Now, place a third peg (preferably of a different colour) between the two and practise clipping over that centre peg.

The idea is to swing through the gate, returning again and again through the slot. Eventually, you will develop that necessary ingredient, the grooved swing.

5A

5B

SIMPLICITY

To simplify your swing, learn to feel where the clubhead is, not where it should be.

The less you think about how to make the swing, the more you will concentrate on actually striking the ball to the target.

Before reaching that happy state, however, there are never-varying factors to be acknowledged and perfected, which is why a great deal of the swing action depends upon the correct set-up or stance. One of the more common problems I encounter in teaching is the way in which many people make an incorrect set-up to the ball.

6A

6B

They set their right hand over the top of the shaft, forcing the right shoulder to ride high. That has the effect of twisting the shoulders open, even though the shaft, feet and hips are all in the correct line. Nobody can make a true swing from a stance like that.

The correct setting is for the right shoulder and elbow to be lower than those on the left. It is important to look at that more closely.

7A

7B

7C

THE STANCE

Many club golfers tend to take for granted after a few years that their stance is, well, alright.

But, if they find their tee shots are not doing what they want, then it is time to get back to basics. Your top pros do it every year—especially at the start of a new season or circuit.

Standing comfortably erect with the arms hanging at the sides, bow from the waist, but keep the back straight (7A). As you tilt, the knees are flexed and the head comes forward about thirty centimetres.

At the other end, (7B, C) the bottom acts as a counter-balance, extending out beyond the heel-line about eight centimetres.

The movement sounds odd, I know, but does not feel that way when done in one, smooth action. You are now ready to set up the club.

Take the correct grip with the left arm extended towards a point halfway between your toes and the ball. The butt of the shaft should now be pointed towards your belt-buckle (7D).

If your right-hand grip is correct, then you will find your right shoulder and elbow below those of the left (7E), but the feet, hips and shoulders are parallel to the intended line of swing (7F). That is very important in terms of attaining accuracy.

OFF THE TEE

Each of us has his own style, but the person who thinks he can forget the basic tenets of the swing is fooling himself. He will never achieve consistent length and accuracy off the tee or fairway.

I have talked earlier about the swing as applied to the shorter irons and the way in which it forms 'the cartwheel effect'. To strike a drive or long shot is to merely extend the various parts of that effect. Yet, it seems to frighten many people. They would rather leave the wood in the bag and take an iron, possibly because they do not trust themselves to get accuracy with the driver.

Whilst it is true that there is more room to impart sidespin in a longer shot, there is no good reason why, if you follow the basic rules of the swing, you can't drive straight. Outside of that, you can be as individual as you like if it is going to help you to play better golf.

Lee Trevino is a very good example of the type of individualist I am thinking of. Lee drives from the tee in a way that stamps him unmistakeably. If that shot is broken down into its various parts, however, you will find a certain standardness about it that is common to all good players. Essentially, while Lee's body may be aligned to the left of the target and his clubface is square to it, he still swings the same way each time—parallel to the target line. The shot goes straight, or whatever shape he wants. Lee pulls the club through with his dominant left side because of a hooded face position at the top.

8A

8B

8C

7D

7E

7F

An incorrect set-up to the ball with the right shoulder riding high.

Many of his colleagues do the same, whereas open-face drivers of the ball have to whip or throw the club through the shot, as I like to do.

As it all begins with the stance, let's look at the basic parts of these longer shots and apply them, in turn, to the driver, the fairway woods and the longer irons.

THE DRIVER

All good golfers have a key thought in their minds, be it a mechanical or a tempo thought, as they tee up for their drives.

They have chosen their target—a bush perhaps, or a hump in the fairway, some identifiable object—and taken their stance in line with it. The eyes are down and concentrating on the back of the ball (8A).

The takeaway begins with that slight forward press of the hands and knees and a kick-start to the movement back. Half-way through, the tempo is reasonably slow, the shoulders coiling and the left arm and shaft in line with the target (8B).

At the top the body weight has shifted to the right leg, but the right knee is remaining flexed to the same amount as it had at the address, while the left is moving in and to the right (8C). Above, the body is fully turned and coiled around a point of centre slightly past the ball, with the left shoulder around and under the chin. At this point, the right elbow has broken down so that it is beneath the shaft, much in the position of a waiter holding a tray of drinks.

The downswing is started with the knees driving towards the target, allowing the shoulders to remain within the line and the clubshaft angled towards the ball (8D).

To reiterate, you start the downward movement with the knees and not the shoulders. It is a feeling that golfers who start with the shoulders are unaware of, and in so doing, they swing from outside the line.

Three-quarters of the way through the action and into the follow-through (8E), the body weight is now well to the left side, but the head and eyes are still over the point where the ball was struck a split-second ago.

Finally, in the completed follow-through (8F), full balance is on the left leg, the knees are together, the right foot has risen on its toe, and the body is facing towards the target. The body weight has revolved fully around to the point of balance and only then does the head turn to follow the ball's flight.

Step-by-step, this is the complete cartwheel action, a totally natural movement aimed at hitting through the ball, driving the clubhead and ball towards the target.

8D

8E

8F

9A

9B

9C

FAIRWAY WOOD

One of the handiest clubs in the bag, the fairway wood is often preferred by some golfers to the driver for getting off the tee.

It is a stick they feel more comfortable with, usually because of its shorter shaft and the more lofted face, although there is only a few degrees difference. Since there is no tee-peg involved in the fairway stroke, the action is one of just brushing the turf with the clubhead, the ball being struck slightly below centre-rear.

The stance with the fairway wood (9A) is much the same as for the driver:

1. The ball slightly inside the left heel.
2. Body weight equal on both legs.
3. Shaft and left arm virtually in a straight line.
4. The hands above the clubhead.

The takeaway starts as a recoil of the forward press of the hands and the slight kick in to the target by the right knee (9B).

The left side coils, (9C) bringing the shoulder around and under the chin so that at the top of the backswing the shoulders have turned about 90 degrees, the hips about 45 degrees, the left heel has risen and the clubshaft is over the right shoulder, pointing to the target (9D).

The start-down (swinging parallel to the stance) is kicked off by the knees driving towards the target, as the left heel is anchoring ready to take the transfer of body weight (9E). The right knee remains inside the line, keeping the shoulders on the same plane.

10A

10B

9D

9E

9F

9G

Naturally, the head remains steady while the weight moves well and truly to the left, the hands releasing and whipping the clubhead through the ball (9F). The arms complete the follow-through with the body facing the target and body weight balanced on the left leg (9G).

THREE-IRON

Although it is basically the same action, the three-iron shot begins with the ball a fraction further back in the stance.

The turf is brushed, or bruised; the clubhead drives down and through, head steady over the centre, and the right hand passing over the left as the arms come through.

Always begin the stroke with that kick in with the right knee, and always start the downswing with the knees, not the shoulders, driving towards the target. (10A–F)

10C

10D

10E

10F

SIX-IRON

As the club-numbers rise, the ball placement moves much nearer the centre and the hands on the shaft are more ahead of the ball.

So too does the backswing become more abbreviated as the club-shafts become shorter.

With the six-iron, the backswing travel is not as far as with the longer irons, but the body coil is just as long (11A–E).

All other factors in the swing are unvarying; head steady, left shoulder comes under the chin, the knees start the downswing drive to the target and the body weight is transferred fully to the left side.

11A

11B

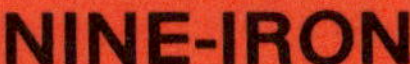

NINE-IRON

The nine-iron is a true utility club, even more so than its nearest cousin, the wedge.

We have seen how useful the nine can be for shorter strokes, the pitches and chips, but it also has a definite role to play in the longer game where

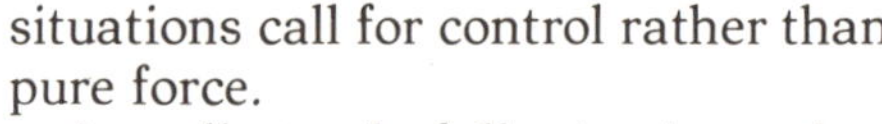

situations call for control rather than pure force.

A well-struck full nine-iron shot should carry the ball about 120 paces, so you can see that it is an extremely handy club to have.

Since the ball is played off centre between the feet with the nine, the hands are ahead, as is body weight, placing the left arm and shaft in a straight line (12A).

With this stance, the backswing becomes sharper, steeper and more compact than for the fuller shots (12B). Yet the left side coil, while still bringing the left shoulder under

12A

12B

12C

11C

11D

11E

the chin, is not quite as long (12C).

More variation here (12D). Half-way through the downswing where the left side is leading the right, hands not yet released, because control in the shot lies with the left arm. A lot of golfers make a mistake with this type of stroke in having the right side out in front of the left, coming down into the ball.

Now comes the release of the hands into the shot (12E). The aim is to pinch the ball, striking down and through and taking a divot, which must be done to collect the ball in the middle of the clubface.

The hands come through with the weight transfer continuing to the point where full balance is held on the left side (12F, G).

Never quit the shot at the vital moment of impact, for what we are aiming for is an accelerating swing and a complete follow-through.

12D

12E

12F

12G

13A

13B

13C

13D

SWEET TIMING

Jane Crafter is a sweet timer of the ball. Her technique has been developed over years of practice and competition.

The key factor in her driving is an excellent weight transference combined with a full backswing.

This is how she does it, step by step:

1. 13A. Comfortably erect at the stance, full extension of the left arm towards the ball, knees slightly flexed.

2. 13B. Wide takeaway with the left shoulder initiating the backswing, left side of the body coiling.

3. 13C. Left side coiling around the centre, shoulder under the chin.

4. 13D. The wrists flex, the club-shaft a fraction past horizontal. The left wrist is flat in a strong position, keeping the clubface up.

5. 13E. The downswing. Right knee travels parallel to the left and both driving along the target line. Shoulders have yet to unwind.

6. 13F. The body uncoiling, hips turning into the shot and body weight driving onto the left leg for the impact. Left arm and shaft in a straight line and the head steady over centre.

7. 13G. Weight transference through the stroke, arms extending down the target line. Head remaining down.

8. 13H. Head comes up, hips facing target fully and weight balanced on left leg at the completion of the follow-through.

SWEEPING IRONS

Jane prefers to sweep her longer iron shots rather than take a divot, just as do many of the top women golfers.

This is a slight disadvantage at times when the lie is a tight one, but on good fairways, the action is very precise and comfortable.

Some years ago, I tried to get Jane to punch down on these shots and over the following months she complained of a sore wrist. It was only when it was X-rayed that a broken

14A

14B

14C

13E

13F

13G

13H

bone was found. Jane had cracked it through punching down into the ball on hard ground.

The incident entrenched in her mind that a sweeping action was a lot safer and more comfortable and that is the way she generally plays all these shots nowadays.

1. 14A. The stance is comfortably erect, the knees flexed. Ball just inside the left heel.
2. 14B. The left shoulder has pushed under the chin, initiating the take-away.
3. 14C. Top of the swing with the left knee in centre. This is the classic 45 degrees of hip turn, and 90 degrees of shoulder turn.
4. 14D. The knees drive towards the target, commencing the down-swing.
5. 14E. Weight transference good, with the left arm and shaft in a straight line and no attempt made to flick the clubhead under the ball.
6. 14F. Knees together having driven through, arms pointed at the target and the head still down.
7. 14G. The completed follow-through with weight fully on the left side.

KNOW YOUR GAME

The hardest thing in golf is to hit the ball straight.

In theory, it should be simple. If you stand straight, swing straight, hit square, then the ball should go straight. It would, too, provided our brains, legs, shoulders, arms, wrists and hands all did exactly the same every time we swung at the ball.

The rules for the perfect drive are simple. There are only three and, in brief, they are:

1. Stand straight, with the body aligned towards the target.
2. Swing parallel to that line.
3. Manipulate the clubhead to keep the ball on the line.

Obviously, there's more to it—all the details involving ball placement, knee action, head steadiness and so on. Basically, however, those three rules are the primary ones for hitting straight.

Where it all goes wrong for the high handicapper, as well as the low,

14D

14E

14F

14G

is in their concentration, the mental effort and attention to detail for making the body and the club do what has to be done.

When they go wrong, the matter becomes one of intelligent observation of the errors and knowing how to correct them.

THE DIAGNOSIS

The majority of ordinary golfers have no idea of what is happening to their clubhead in the swing. The professionals do and that is the difference between them; they know simply because they watch the ball in flight. All other factors being equal, the ball's flight tells them when they have either manipulated the clubhead incorrectly, failed to swing along the target line, or both.

Through one or both of these errors, there are four common shots of misdirection. The photograph illustrates:

1. A straight hit to left of target, which is a pull shot.
2. The same shot, but the ball curving away to the right.
3. The opposite—the ball heading away to right of target which is a push-shot.
4. The same shot, plus the ball swerving to the left in flight.

So, each of the shots starts off line; two of them continue straight right and straight left and the other two curve back across the line—the hook and the slice.

The highest percentage of golfers slice their drives. If you tend to hook, then you are almost certainly a better-than-average golfer.

Whichever you do, your action requires diagnosis and correction, and this can be done only on the practice fairway.

The initial task is to check your alignment. Place a club on the ground with the shaft lined up precisely on a conspicuous target at the other end of the fairway. Throughout the routine, the shaft will be between the ball and your feet.

Set yourself in a comfortable stance, parallel to a line running from the shaft to the target. If your shoulders are properly aligned, you should be looking at the target over the left shoulder. In fact, you can make sure by picking up the club and laying it across the throat so that each end of the shaft is touching the shoulders, allowing you to look naturally down the line to the target.

It is common for people to think that their stance is square when, in

fact, while their hips and legs may be parallel to the line, their shoulders are open. This gives their swing an outside-in line. Nicklaus and Trevino do this, but obviously they know what they are doing and compensate, whereas the average person is unaware that he even has a problem.

Now, having checked the stance alignment, start hitting balls down the fairway towards the target and carefully note their flight patterns. This is how to diagnose your problem.

THE SLICE

You have observed that the ball consistently curves away to the right. You have sliced the shot but, rather than doing what seems to be obvious and trying to swing correctly, what needs to be done first is to produce the opposite curve in the shot.

1. Control the clubface angle by adjusting the grip—twisting the vees in the hands to the right—and hood the blade back and down in the swing.
2. Hit a few more balls and experment to learn how much hooding the blade needs to start the ball left of the target line instead of the right.
3. Now, adjust the swing line to an inside-out action, exaggerating the adjustment at first. The ball's flight again will show you how much or how little exaggeration is taking place and consequently, how much adjustment is needed to bring the swing line parallel with the target line.

THE HOOK

The less common error is the hook where the ball curves away to the left.

Correcting this has the same basic factors: first control the clubface angle and then adjust the swing-line.

1. Weaken the grip if necessary to open the clubface, producing a deliberate slice to counteract the hook. The ball will start out right of target now and continue that way without the curve.
2. Adjust the swing-line through an exaggerated outside-in action, experimenting and adjusting with each stroke until you have the ball starting out down the target line.

CARTWHEELS AND SWING LINES

With all these forceful shots, it is important that the right elbow be below the left.

If it is not (and this is common) then the right shoulder will be out and on top, the right arm straight and higher than the left. That posture automatically sets up for a swing line across the body.

Once you have that right elbow correct, you can start looking at the shape of your swing line, which is the direction our arms and shoulders travel in hitting the ball.

Your natural swing wants to do something that *you* do not, so it has to be trained. And only the ball's flight can tell you what needs to be done. The most effective way is to *over*-correct.

Ask yourself: 'Did the ball start out on the target line?'

If not, then adjust the swing line. Perhaps the club has to be swung more inside the line to hit out. *Or*, if the case is opposite, the club may have to start out more from the body and then brought back across it.

Both are exaggerated swings and are clearly wrong. Yet you have to be prepared to practise, observe and make adjustments within those two extremes until you strike a balance which will give you a parallel swing line.

All this is merely making use of your eyes and brain. You aim at a target and if the ball does not start heading for it, then your cartwheel effect is not parallel to where you stood.

To swing straight, the cartwheel has to be aligned in both dimensions. **Vertically** towards the ball, it is aligned through your neck and chest, which is the operative centre of your swing or the cartwheel's hub. And then, the **horizontal** diameter of the wheel must also be aligned towards the target.

There will be very few balls that will go exactly straight but many of the less than perfect shots will be very acceptable.

To sum up (in order of importance) the rules are:

1. **Stand straight, aligned to the target.**
2. **Swing parallel to that line.**
3. **Manipulate the clubface to keep the ball on that line.**

THE WRIST ACTION

If your swing line is corrected and provided you are hitting the ball with a square blade, then the ball will stay on line.

But when the ball curves off at the end of its flight, either right or left, then you have to adjust the movement of the hands and forearms to bring that blade square at the moment of impact.

Always, that curve at the end of flight seems to prevent a person from swinging correctly. Because of it, they think they have to again adjust their swing and this usually causes them to hit the ball a glancing blow. They lose force which they can least afford to do.

Ninety per cent of golf books will tell you that looping and swinging outside-in will cause a slice. In truth, it is the other way around.

The open clubface causes the slice and that then induces the golfer to swing outside-in to allow for it. Naturally, the problem only becomes worse. I have seen it happen hundreds of times with pupils. They set the

15A

15B

clubface square to begin, make a copy-book backswing, then fail to realise that on return to the ball the clubface is approaching side-on, 90 degrees open. This downswing clubface angle is correct. But not knowing this, they then flick the wrist forward instead of twisting the forearms to square the face. This twist is not a natural action and must be trained.

The hooker's problem usually stems from the wrong grip and this allows the excessive twisting down of the clubface at impact. The right arm twists over the left and, as a result, the ball is hooked away to the left.

That flick (in the slice) and that incorrect crossover (in the hook) have to be replaced with the correct amount of forearm twist, about 45 degrees' worth.

The first exercise (15A, B) is designed to teach the type of wrist action you use in taking the club back to the top of the swing.

Take the correct grip and hold the club out at shoulder-height, making a vertical flexing of the wrists so that the club is raised at a right angle.

Keep doing that, moving the wrists up and down (never to the sides) and letting the right elbow flex as you do it. The exercise should be done regularly, about ten to twelve times each session, to demonstrate and instill the basic shape of the correct wrist action in the backswing. It will train your left arm to remain straight (always a bogey for golfers) as you flex your wrists against it.

The next exercise (16A–C) has the purpose of teaching you to whip the clubhead past the left arm in a horizontal or flat semi-circular movement.

First, raise the clubhead to vertical then twist it across until it is lying horizontal. Now, you exercise that wrist action, keeping the left arm quite firm and straight. Straighten out the wrists and twist the club to square.

From side-on, the clubface twists up so that it is vertical. This virtually is the point of impact with the ball. Keep the left arm firm and make the forearms crossover so that the clubface is then facing the ground. This is the forearm twisting I spoke of to get the clubface square coming into the impact zone.

In all, the clubface moves through 180 degrees—90 degrees up to square, then a further 90 degrees off line.

16A

16B

16C

The final exercise (17A–C) gives you the correct wrist action in the swing and allows you to note (in virtual slow-motion) what the clubhead actually does in striking the ball. Most people do not know *where* the clubhead is in their swing, let alone *what* it does.

First, the clubface is vertical or side-on, 90 degrees off line to the target.

Now, besides straightening the wrists you have to twist the forearms to square the face, then bring it back to vertical.

In the actual swing, the face is vertical approaching the ball in the downward movement. It straightens out with the forearm twist, then continues around until it is again vertical.

In this twisting movement, the left hand and forearm have to be trained to dominate. An excellent way to do this is to swing the club and exercise with the left hand only gripping. Do it slowly, however, to watch the angles of the clubface, twisting face down as you hit to stop slicing—twisting face-up to stop hooking.

TIMING

It is almost as if Nature has gone out of her way to make life difficult for golfers. Once you have these wrist and arm movements correct, there is still the question of timing.

In hitting a golf ball straight and far, there are, in fact, two different areas of timing.

The first is 'contact timing'.

This involves collecting the ball in the club's 'sweet spot', the exact centre of the face and we've talked about that in the training routine using the three tee-pegs.

The second is 'tempo timing'.

This is greatly affected by the speed of the body turn through the stroke and that left-handed training I just mentioned is good for rehearsing this, by making full swings, learning to

17A

17B

17C

hit balls left-arm only, in slow-motion.

Tempo timing involves locating the correct wrist and forearm twist in the vital part of the downswing—through the impact zone. The twist must take place halfway through the downswing and be completed halfway along the follow-through.

If the action takes place earlier, even though the twist is done correctly, the result will be a hooked drive.

If it comes too late, then the result will be a slice.

You have to get this tempo timing right or else all the previous work you have done on the wrists, forearms and swing line will be for nothing.

As a final observation on the subject of swing lines, it is interesting that some good golfers do make adjustments by aiming left. Nicklaus and Trevino allow for an inside-out or push-to-the-right stroke, but I cannot think of a single champion who has done the opposite.

For perfection in swing lines, one doesn't have to go past Peter Thomson. He has always stood immaculately square to the target and swung down that line. And because he knows what happens to his clubhead in the swing, he can draw or fade the shot whenever the situation demands.

While all of this makes Thommo not only a great golfer in terms of the textbook, do not forget that he is also an imaginative shot-maker.

I have also heard and read a lot about Ben Hogan and what a super player he was. Yet, somehow, when I balance the factors out, I think I would still put Trevino up against him and collect money. For Lee, you see, is a thinking golfer, and despite all that baloney he comes up with, is one of the few *real* golfers left in the world. To Lee, orthodoxy does not count, and he possesses what I call 'a good pair of hands'—hands that enable him to bring out an astonishing range of strokes simply because he knows exactly what he is doing. A true professional.

Shearer's Eighteenth

EIGHTEENTH, THE AUSTRALIAN GC—
PAR FIVE, 459 METRES

The Australian Golf Club layout in Sydney has been called 'unforgiving'. But, then I don't know of many championship courses that aren't. It is hard to remain objective about the Australian, perhaps because of all the great changes it has undergone in recent years, courtesy of Kerry Packer.

But the Australian Open played there in 1982 will live long in the memory of those who saw it. This was Bob Shearer's Championship and his play over those four days was a little out of character for him. Instead of the boldness with which he normally plays, Shearer took the course nice and easy, was patient and collected the birdies as they came.

On the last day, he could have lost it all at the Eighth and Fourteenth when he had to scramble out of potential bogey situations. Yet, it was his play on the Eighteenth which most people remember.

Perhaps it was because of the Eighteenth's perfect setting for a championship finish—a natural amphitheatre filled with thousands of spectators. Perhaps it was because he held a four-stroke lead going to the Eighteenth that brought a return of Shearer's normal dash and boldness, hitting a superb iron to the heart of the green when he could have so easily laid up safe with his second.

Whatever it was on that day, the Eighteenth at the Australian remains a super par five finisher.

Carrying the lake extending out in front of the green is a lovely temptation for those long hitters who think the shortcut could save a stroke coming home. Be warned; after a mentally-eroding round on a tough course, you have to be a Shearer with a four-stroke lead to even think about it.

The ordinary golfer here should try to play his tee shot as accurately and as safely as he can. Perhaps the three-wood might serve better than the driver, for the aim is to lay up short of the left-hand fairway traps. Teeing up on the right-hand side will provide a bigger margin for error for the right-hand bunkers really are horrors.

The second shot could be either a four-iron or four-wood, the aim being to lay up short of the lake. Shearer, incidentally, took a three-iron for this shot, carrying another 100 metres on to the green.

Third shot—a nine-iron, flighting over the lake's edge to the left of the green. On the right, the lake curves around the three tiers. With the flag set back, there is no slope from this lie so the putt is a simple crossways one.

Once you have holed out, you will know a little of the feeling Shearer had that day of having played a great course and a great Eighteenth.

A Watery Hazard

FOURTEENTH, THE LAKES GC, SYDNEY—PAR FIVE, 495 METRES

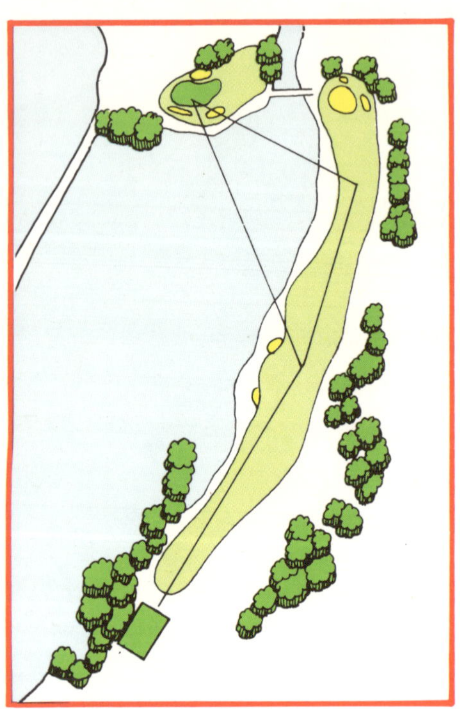

If golf is to be regarded as a test of character, then the Fourteenth at the Lakes Club in Sydney must provide one of the game's ultimate trials.

It is a famous hole. Television made it so in the ABC coverage of the 1980 Australian Open which was played over the course and won by Greg Norman from Brian Jones.

Apart from anything else, the Fourteenth provokes three questions for the ordinary golfer.

1. Can you hit straight?
2. How much faith do you have in your judgement of distances over water?
3. How confident are you in being able to hit those distances?

Let's take the first question. Off the tee, you cannot go left—there is water all the way. There is not much joy on the right, either, with plenty of sand, pines, scrubby wattles, boobiallas and thick, wiry grass. The answer obviously is that you must hit straight, or suffer the penalties.

What was it that Dr Johnson said? 'Nothing concentrates the mind so wonderfully as the threat of hanging.' Perhaps in another age he might have been thinking of the Fourteenth at the Lakes.

By the way, this is an unusual hole in that it has two greens. The first is in a direct line off the tee for the ladies. The second is a dog-leg left over the lake and onto a narrow neck of land.

Which brings me to the second question. You have a choice for second shot. If you think you can estimate distance over water and then hit that length, then you could try to emulate Greg Norman and the other big boys and take the short-cut over water. The thousands of balls beneath the water (including two struck by our photographer Roger Gould) are testimony to the attempts which failed.

The other choice for second shot is the safest. A three or four-iron down towards the ladies' green, about 200 paces, then an eight-iron to the green. At least for this shot, the golfer can pace off his distance. I don't know of any golfer who can walk on water, although there are some who think they can.

Putting on the Fourteenth is not simple either, for there are some tricky slopes to negotiate.

All in all, a one over par at the Lakes' Fourteenth can bring a very satisfactory result—and always a big sigh of relief.

The Deceiver

FIRST, THE GRANGE WEST COURSE, ADELAIDE—PAR FIVE, 464 METRES

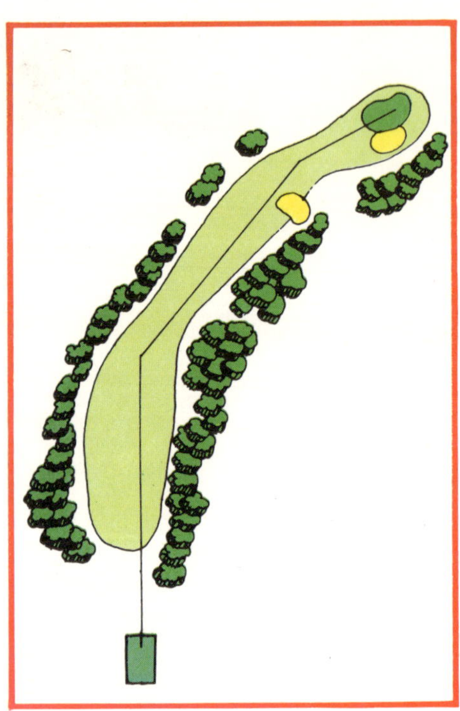

After those other two driving holes, the First on Adelaide's Grange West Course seems to be a change of pace.

There is nothing terribly difficult about the First. Not a drop of water in sight, it is immaculately groomed—a nice, pleasant opening hole with acres of fairway.

The trouble is that it can tend to lure the golfer into a false sense of security. After the First, the Grange gets to be much harder.

It is a great driver's hole. Off the tee, the golfer can be very confident with over 460 metres of country ahead of him. There is hardly an obstacle in view if he is reasonably straight.

For the ladies, it is much the same. Their distance here is 441 metres and in playing the First, Jane and I can look forward to the same rewards as do many members at the Grange.

With the fairway so beautifully manicured, there cannot be a bad lie around for second shots and anybody can take delight in playing their fairway wood in ideal conditions.

The only possible trouble comes closer in to the green where there are sand traps on the right-hand side. In such surroundings, they seem to be there only for effect, to round out the picture of a perfect opening hole. For the men, the third shot should be a seven-iron, for the ladies, an eight. For the long hitters, the distinct possibility of an eagle putt is a great temptation to gamble.

Putting, too, is a pleasure with the green always given lots of attention by the ground-staff.

The idea with the First at the Grange is to plan and strive for a par, with the likelihood that if you are on your form, a birdie is a possible result for diligence expended.

Only, take a little more care and patience with the next seventeen holes.

One of the celebrated holes in Australian golf, the Fourteenth at the Lakes. A water carry is mandatory—with the second shot for the brave and skilful, and the third shot for the average player.

6 Recovery Shots

The theory goes that to play winning golf, one has to play the percentages: keep out of trouble.

Unfortunately, golf shots are not always played off flat lies, from short grass and with no obstacles on the way to the green. So, any golfer aspiring to greater things must have the mental approach, training and techniques to get himself out of trouble.

The conservative golfer often becomes more intent on not failing rather than winning. He knows all the shots, standard though they be, and if he misses a fairway, he simply makes a standard recovery shot. It makes for low scores, but hardly for excitement.

Fortunately for golf and for us, there are players willing to use imagination and flair. And when the conversation gets around to the subject of trouble shots, one name comes up, first and always—Spain's Seve Ballesteros.

Whereas others try to stay out of the rough stuff, Seve seems to take delight in getting into it. That brings out tens of thousands of golfing fans whenever he tees up in a tournament. They can relate to the way in which Seve plays because they get into the same kind of trouble.

All the excitement over his exploits tends to mask the fact that he plays one of the best all-round games in the world. His driving is powerful, his fairway shots immaculate and his short game is marked by a marvellous delicacy. Why he stands above other golfers in the recovery zone is because of the sound basis to his game and the imagination he brings to this part of golf.

Ballesteros is an example in the way he thinks long and hard about each shot, his endeavour to seek the most promising escape route and his calmness of outlook.

The best-known Ballesteros exploit would have to be his recovery shot from the car park at Royal Lytham and St Anne's after a misdirected tee shot during the 1979 British Open. In fact, he hit only about half the fairways on his way to the title.

Another incident was at the US Masters the following year. His drive off the Seventeenth tee travelled all of 300 metres to a perfect landing . . . on the Seventh green! Taking a drop, he calmly pitched over a course scoreboard to the Seventeenth green and then holed a dreadfully long putt for a birdie!

Both events added to Ballesteros' reputation as the world's luckiest golfer. But he believes that on the golf course, a person makes his own luck through sound play. The point about his waywardness off the tee in the above cases is that he knew exactly what he had to do to recover. Not everyone can be a Ballesteros. As Hogan, Nicklaus and others maintain, stay out of trouble as best you can. But, if you do land in it, you should know what to do about the problem, be it a tight lie in a divot or a more awkward one behind a tree.

1

2A

2B

2C

2D

3

4A

4B

4C

4D

On the following pages, we have outlined the more common forms of trouble and the techniques required to escape. There is nothing mysterious about them; in one way or another, all are variations on the basic themes of playing straightforward shots. But, they do require observation, thinking and planning.

PLAYING FROM LONG GRASS

When playing out of long grass—by long, I mean anything over the ankles—the aim is to make as much distance with the shot as possible. Flight and loft are the keys. With a straight-faced club, the ball will tend to come out low after fighting its way through the grass, so you should use a club with more loft than you apparently need.

The ball is played off centre (1) with the clubface twisted open in a slicer's grip, much as with the sand iron in a bunker. However, the grip is a tight one, the club literally being squashed with pressure applied on the last three fingers of the left hand.

2E

The grip has to be tight. For one thing, the club's neck is going to be grabbed by the grass to some extent, especially if it's that wiry stuff found in the rough on some courses. For another, when the club is grabbed the grass will tend to flick the face closed and take the loft off the shot.

The swing is a full one (2A–E). The wrists break sharply in the backswing to bring the club down to strike very hard about seven centimetres behind the ball so as to get the clubface underneath. Don't worry too much about follow-through . . . with most types of grass there won't be much anyway.

A general thought to keep in mind is to aim to get the ball up quickly out of the grass with a full swing and make it travel a respectable distance.

Only experience will tell you what shot to play in the various types of grasses and their heights, and what amount of loft you will need to get out of them. If you are in doubt, sacrifice distance for loft. If you think the shot calls for a seven-iron, better to use the nine. As with all shots in golf, this type of situation calls for logical observation and a decision made on the facts.

PLAYING FROM LOW SCRUB

This sequence of photographs was taken at Royal Melbourne where the scrub is ti-tree, very branchy and very tough. If you find yourself in this sort of scrub, don't claim an unplayable lie if you know in your heart that it is not. Have a go at it. The rewards will be greater than if you had backed off.

This particular shot calls for a nine-iron and like any other club in this situation it can be wrenched out of the fingers. Hold on tightly, leaning on the left leg and setting the clubface open with the hands well in front (3).

Obviously, the swing is a very full, hard one where you chop down sharply, trusting the loft in the clubhead. The crucial factors are:

1. Hold on tightly with the left hand and arm to counteract the shock and resistance of the trees.
2. Keep the clubface open to allow for the scrub grabbing at it, flipping it closed (4A–D).

This shot, incidentally, made about fifty paces out of the scrub.

THE SPINNING FLIP SHOT

A bunker, deep and yawning, lies between you and the green, yet the shot has to be one of only eight paces. Truly a trap, and to go round will cost strokes.

How many times have you found yourself in this situation? And how many times have you got out of it only to see the ball fly through the back of the green?

The answer to the problem is the spinning flop shot, one of golf's little treasures. Executed well, it can cut strokes off your score.

5A

5B

Primarily, the lie must be quite good with sufficient grass under the ball to allow the clubface to slide through, in a sense cutting the legs from under the ball.

A divot is not to be taken because that will deprive the ball of lift which, rather than backspin, is the main stopping effect. The ball needs to be got up quickly to give it vertical fall potential. If you do that, the ball will virtually stop dead, even on the rockiest green.

The shot should be taken with a sand iron, preferably one without a big flange. I liken the spinning flop to an exaggeration of the green-side bunker shot, only taken off grass and struck cleanly.

The grip is weak and very soft, arms hanging like straps from the shoulders, for basically you are swinging the weight of the clubhead through with minimum acceleration. For such a short shot, the stroke is long and slow—say a three-quarter swing at half-force. If you want more distance, don't hit harder, merely take a longer swing.

Here, I am aiming ten to twelve paces to the left of the flag and the clubface is twisted open in a slicer's grip to aim about the same distance to the right. Emphasising the technique, (5A, B) the idea is for the ball to be flipped with the wrists hingeing; the left arm stops almost at the point of impact, allowing the clubhead to pass through, the right hand going underneath the left, keeping the clubface open.

Body weight begins at the address balanced on both feet equally, and then moves forward with the shot.

Now, some people teach that in all shots you should keep your head down. That's right. But what I would like to emphasise as well, particularly in these short shots, is that you should keep your KNEES DOWN, without minimising the importance of watching the point of contact with the ball. So, here (6A–F) the knees are fairly loose, as are the arms. The knees remain bent throughout the shot, rolling a little as you swing forward and helping the whole movement towards sliding the clubhead under the ball.

You will keep your body down if you retain a constant knee bend throughout the stroke.

Instead of trying to keep your head down, keep your knees down.

As I said, the spinning flip shot is an exaggeration of the trap shot, and much favoured by the pros. That does not mean that you shouldn't have it in *your* bag of shots. A true recovery stroke.

6A

6B

6C

THE EXPLOSION

If your lie is not good behind the bunker, or if the grass is a bit long, then the situation demands not a flip shot, but an explosion. Simply, it is a bunker shot off grass.

Focus seven to eight centimetres behind the ball, open the clubface, lean slightly more on the left leg, break the wrists sharply in the backswing and belt into the grass harder than you would for a trap shot.

It takes courage to do that, but it is well worth a try. You know you cannot play a chip from this type of lie as the ball would probably land in the trap. There is little, if any, backspin in this explosion approach. The ball comes out like one which has been buried in the sand. Off grass, the divot you take obviously does not dissipate as sand does and, as a consequence, the ball is virtually spinless.

OUT OF WATER

There is enough water on Australian golf courses to warrant learning the technique of getting out of it. The Lakes and the Australian clubs, both in Sydney, are two that come readily to mind.

The old theory of not attempting to play when the ball is fully submerged is still the safest. When the ball is more than its depth under water, then I regard the shot as being not on. But if the ball is showing the slightest amount above water level, then go ahead.

Remember don't touch the water at address—penalty.

The technique is the same as for the long trap shot, i.e. a full explosion shot, the club being picked up sharply in the backswing and struck down forcefully seven to eight centimetres behind the ball.

FROM SANDY GRASS OVER BUNKER

The lie here is much the same as on the previous page, except that the grass is thin. The situation demands not a flip shot, but an explosion from this sandy waste grass (7).

The ball cannot be taken cleanly because of the risk of belting through the back of the green, and so needs to be taken with the club's point of entry about three centimetres behind.

The stance line is about five paces to the left and the clubface opened to aim the same distance to the right.

7

6D

6E

6F

8A

8B

8C

Again, using the sand iron in a three-quarter swing, the wrists break sharply and the body kept down as it moves through the shot; the right side comes well through (8A–F).

In that sandy waste, the ball will have a great deal of backspin and allowance must be made for it.

If, however, the grass was thicker, there would be little backspin as the ball would come out with a lot of sand and grass.

CHIPPING FROM BAD LIE

Competency in these shots can be achieved if you aim the clubface properly, align the body correctly and swing along the stance-line.

The job of hitting to a target becomes much harder when the ball is in a divot or a pockety lie near the green. It takes a sharp chop down to get the ball out so the shot requires a change in touch from the normal chip and only you can decide how much is required.

With that action, using a six or seven-iron, the ball will shoot out horizontally and run too far. Try the nine or the wedge and the loft on these clubs will at least give the ball a chance of getting some lift and thus shortening the run across the green.

Play the ball back in your stance towards the right foot (9A) still keeping the body weight leaning about 70 per cent to the left so that your hands are in front of the club-head.

The club is lifted sharply, the wrists breaking, and the downward movement is a quick stab right at the back of the ball (9B, C). The ball will squirt out much like a five or six-iron chip.

As in all shots, watch where the ball *was* for a split longer than you are used to doing, looking up only after the ball is well and truly on its way.

UPHILL AND DOWN

THE DOWNSLOPE

With a lie that is not level, you must have a fair idea before you start of how the ball will fly from the type of shot you have to play.

9A

9B

8D

8E

8F

The basic rule is that you will tend to hook from an uphill lie and slice from one on a downslope. So, allow for these different flights in the way in which you set yourself for the shot.

Don't try to change your normal swing; align your body instead to allow for the ball-flight pattern.

For example, in playing an iron shot off a downslope, you are going to lose loft, probably as much as three clubs' worth. A five-iron shot will fly like a two-iron, and a seven like a four. But, what you lose in loft you will gain in distance; therefore be acutely aware of any obstacles in front of you.

In a downslope stance, (10) set yourself relatively well-balanced. The right knee is broken slightly more than normal and the weight is predominantly on the left leg.

The idea is to follow the slope with the swing. The club is brought up in the backswing more sharply than usual; then you hit down and forward, skimming the turf and following the angle of the slope with the backswing.

9C

10

UPSLOPE WITH WOOD OR LONG IRON

Obviously, from this position you are looking for maximum distance in the shot.

It will pay, therefore, to have a few practice swings, for while the normal tendency is to dig the club into the hill, you must follow the slope with the arc of the club. A few rehearsals will give you the feeling for the stroke.

Ball placement is not greatly different from normal and while the stance (11) is square to the slope, the angle means that you will be playing off the right leg which is supporting most of the body weight. In turn, this alters the swing line to a lower, wider one so again I stress the need for those practice swings before taking the address.

11

UPSLOPE WITH SHORT IRON

The uphill shot is much the same with a short iron where you want excessive height to put the ball down onto a heavily trapped green. Again, set yourself square to the slope and swing so that you follow that angle.

However, if the target is open and there is not the demand for loft in the shot, you will gain extra control by punching the ball. This is done by leaning into the slope and driving the clubhead into the ground (12). The swing will come to an abrupt finish, of course, and the ball will punch out but, as I said, you will find yourself in more control of the shot.

13A

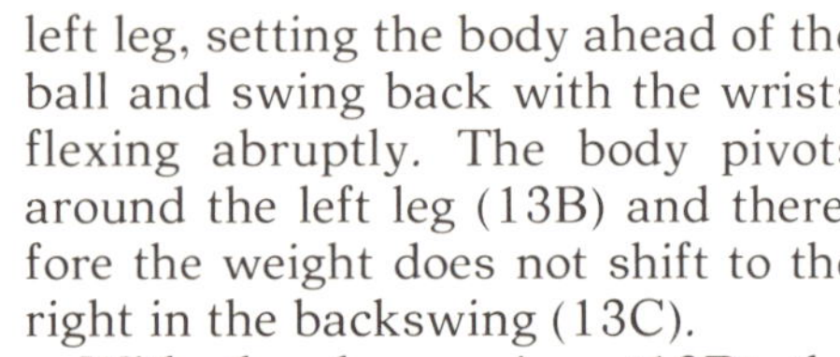

13B

12

BALL IN DIVOT

One of the more annoying trouble spots on any golf course is the divot hole. Perhaps it is because you know that the hole is the result of someone's carelessness in not replacing the divot.

Still, your ball is in it and must be played from there. Depending on how deep the hole is, you must use a well-lofted club, nothing less than an eight, nine or wedge. In these photographs, the divot hole is very deep, calling for a nine-iron.

In playing the shot, the first temptation for many people is to try to bury the clubhead in the back of the ball and get it out by brute force. That is a mistake. The aim is to squeeze it out with a sharp, chopping stroke, making no attempt to lift the ball but allowing the clubface loft to do that part of the job.

In the stance, (13A) lean onto the left leg, setting the body ahead of the ball and swing back with the wrists flexing abruptly. The body pivots around the left leg (13B) and therefore the weight does not shift to the right in the backswing (13C).

With the downswing, (13D) the idea is to pull down sharply with the heel of the left hand, dragging the butt of the grip down towards the ball. This produces the chopping action needed to play the ball out.

14A

14B

13C

13D

13E

The follow-through (13E) will be very short, very abrupt. Trust the loft on the blade to obtain what height there is available out of the hole.

The shot is an effective one. The ball will come out low and fast and run for some distance, so anticipate this. For example, you are turning a nine-iron into a five as far as height is concerned. Rehearse the shot on the practice fairway. You will find no shortage of divot holes there. Most golfers, when practising, keep setting the ball on the highest tuft of grass they can find, almost never testing these tight lies, and so are poorly prepared for this situation when it comes.

SIDE-SLOPE LIES

Just as with an uphill or downhill lie, the shot played from the side of a slope will tend to spin off line ahead, and must be allowed for.

The general rule is that the flight will follow the direction of the slope. For the lie above the feet, the ball will curve away to the left while the one below the feet will slice to the right. Another factor to be aware of is that a sidehill lie will force an alteration to your stance.

BALL ABOVE FEET

An awkward lie such as the one in the photographs will make for an extremely flat swing, in fact almost at waist-height. That means the clubface will be closed on contact with the ball, which is a difficult thing to avoid and in 90 per cent of cases the aim will have to be to the right.

Practice swings will give you the feeling for the shot, which calls for the clubface to just skim the grass and not dig into it.

The body is fairly erect at the stance and throughout the stroke (14A–D) because of the height of the ball on the slope. Do not stand further away from the ball, as many people think they should do. Simply choke the hands down the handle almost to the bottom of the grip, and make the shot allowing for the flatter swing pulling the ball left.

14C

14D

BALL BELOW FEET

This seems as if it should be a distorted shot, but it need not be. The natural tendency with the ball below foot level is to push the body back on the heels and bend further than one would normally.

The secret, however, is to take a normal stance, body naturally balanced on the balls of the feet. Then, instead of bending the back more, simply go down from the knees. This gives you the chance to stay level with the ball and to swing without distortion. Look at the sequence of photographs (15A–E). I am taking the usual stance but addressing fresh air about thirty centimetres above the ball.

Next, I flex the knees to get the body down and *keep them flexed* right through the stroke. This is played normally, hitting down and through the ball. In the follow-through (15E) the knees remain distinctly bent which really is the key to playing this shot well. The error tendency is to catch the ball with the shank or to slice it badly.

Thus, rehearsal swings are essential to enable you to get used to the feeling of playing at this unusual height. The aim is to the left to counteract the slice problem.

FLYING HIGH—OVER TREES

While this shot is aimed at getting you over trees or other tall obstacles, the technique involved is the one Jack Nicklaus uses for all his iron shots. He, like the other top pros, looks for height to get the ball to stop quickly.

I do not recommend it for all iron shots by the average golfer for it requires, in the longer irons, very strong wrists, a fast-driving leg action and plenty of practice. That's alright for Nicklaus, of course, since he spends most of his life playing that way.

But, to get over trees with say, a seven-iron, it is the technique you must bring into play to obtain height. Simply, the club has to be slipped and flicked under the ball and when struck correctly there will be no loss of distance but certainly a gain in height.

Key factors are to play the ball off the left heel and to open the clubface slightly to counteract the resulting tendency to hook.

Here, (16A) I am using the seven-iron and the body weight is about equal on both feet, possibly a shade towards the right leg. But, the hands at the address are behind the ball since the intention is to take the ball

15A

15B

16A

16B

15C

15D

15E

at the lowest point of the swing arc, almost on the rise.

In making the backswing, (16B, C) the body weight is transferred fully onto the right leg and at the top, the club is over the shoulder and pointing slightly left of the target.

Now, swing down keeping the back foot well planted for balance (16D) and do not move onto the left leg as you would in playing a normal seven-iron shot. Keep the weight back on that right leg and hit through the ball at the bottom of the swing (16E).

The idea is to take a low, skimming divot. At first, the likelihood will be to catch the ball either too fat or too thin, but with a little practice you will soon find that you can flick it up quite firmly with this stroke.

To sum up:

Ball off the left heel.

Weight on the back leg.

Clubface opened slightly.

Keep the right foot planted on the ground through the shot.

Body weight in behind the shot.

Take the ball at the lowest point of the swing.

16C

16D

16E

FLYING LOW—UNDER TREES

This is said to be Ballesteros' favourite. I am not positive about that myself, but he certainly is adept at getting out from under trees.

A virtual shut-down shot, it is played in a similar way to when the wind is in your face. The ball obviously has to be kept low, so you should do some work on the technique on the practice fairway with the straighter-faced clubs. That way you will learn what trajectories you are likely to get. Once you are under trees out on the course, it is too late to try and find out.

The ball is played back in the stance, but the weight is on the left side. By pivoting around the left leg at the top of the swing, you will keep the body ahead of the ball and ensure collecting the ball before you collect turf (17A).

The next two photographs (17B, C) show the correct wrist action—the left wrist and arm particularly are held up under the strain of hitting down sharply and do not collapse.

This is one of the factors necessary for keeping the ball down; that your hands stay well ahead of the club, the back of the left turning down and the arm and shaft not in a straight line at the point of impact (17D).

Do that and you will get your recovery every time.

17A

17B

FAIRWAY TRAPS

The technique for recovery from fairway traps is quite different to that from green-side traps. Select a club with sufficient loft to clear the bunker lip. In so doing, you should realise that a shot from a fairway trap will usually come out two clubs lower than one played off a turf lie with the same club.

18A

18B

18C

17C

17D

So, if you think you can recover with a six-iron, better to use the eight; if you believe a four-wood will get the ball up and out, then it will be safer to use the four or five-iron.

The standard technique has the aim of pinching the ball out of the sand, not scooping it; that is usually fatal.

In the stance (18A):

The ball is played just backward of centre.

The clubface is square to the target-line.

Your feet must have a firm grip in the sand.

The hands are ahead of centre.

Body weight is more on the left leg than normal.

This setup will enable you to hit down sharply and collect the ball, with a minimum of sand, *before* the lowest point of the swing. That emphasises the need for sufficient loft to the club you have selected.

In the backswing (18B, C) the shoulders turn, but the body weight remains on the left with the head still ahead of the ball. This ensures that the bottom of the arc will be *beyond* the ball.

Shifting through the shot (18D) body weight leads quite considerably, the head still in front of the ball as the club comes down sharply (18E) collecting the ball an instant before collecting sand.

The follow-through should be full and wide with no surrendering to the temptation to hold back on the shot (18F).

This technique should suit most lies in a bunker on the fairway and punch the ball not far short of your normal distance. Remember, though, that the aim is to get the ball out of the bunker without wasting strokes; better to leave the ball short of the green than to leave it in the bunker with a badly-planned and executed stroke. These shots can be played as

18D

18E

18F

19A

19B

19C

per the high-flying iron shot used by some top pros if the lie is good enough, but at great risk. Experiment before trying this in match conditions.

AROUND TREES

Once you hit into the woods, your chances of getting out of the problem are increased if you stay calm rather than becoming agitated.

Observe the situation logically and select the shot which will give you not only the best escape route but also put you in the best possible position for the next shot.

Use your imagination. If you cannot play a normal stroke, fashion one.

Here, (19A) the ball is absolutely full against the butt of the tree. No normal swing is possible, so I have turned the face of the club down for a little two-handed chop shot. Sometimes, this can be played between the legs or you can do it alongside as I am doing.

The next two photographs show two different methods of handling the same situation. In the first (19B) you can play the ball one-handed from alongside the tree, especially if you are predominantly right-handed.

Or, you can try it left-handed (19C).

Whichever way you choose, the basic aim is to get the ball clear and set up as well as possible for the next shot. With these kinds of rather back-handed recoveries, by just skimming the ground with the clubface you can play the shot out for up to fifty paces. Good contact is everything and you should literally *stare* at the point of contact.

CONTROLLED HOOK

In looking for the best escape route from trouble, do not be restricted by the obvious.

If, for example, a large tree on fairway left is directly between you

20A

20B

20C

and the green, don't try to get over or through if there is a likelihood of rebounding off a branch.

Try going around the tree, bending right to left to get back into play if not close to the green, at least on the fairway and thus set up for a direct shot to the flag.

In effect, the shot is a controlled hook, the use of an otherwise incorrect technique in an imaginative yet deliberate way to escape from trouble.

It starts with setting the grip (20A) to keep the clubface closed to produce the necessary right-to-left spin on the ball. There is a shift in the grip in that the hands are twisted so that the vees are pointing outside the right shoulder, but the clubface is held square.

In making the backswing, (20B) the hands revert almost to their normal position, enabling you to hold the clubface tilted down at least 45 degrees waist-high in the takeaway.

Now the movement requires practice, especially just before taking the actual address. In these rehearsals, stop half-way through the takeaway, about waist-high, and check to see that the clubface is tilted down; then swing through, waist to waist to ensure that your hands are working correctly in this position (20C). You have what is called a hooker's grip, which although does not guarantee a hook, facilitates the action.

The most crucial part of the whole stroke lies in the swing line and stance.

There is a common belief in teaching that to hook, a golfer has to close his stance and swing inside-out. That is not so. You just set your stance along the line of aim, in this case, towards a point away to the right where you want the ball to start out before the hook takes over. Instead of drawing the right foot back in a closed stance (which tends to pull the shoulders off line), align your body along the aiming line and then swing parallel to it (21A–D).

It is difficult to hit a high hook shot, for the action will close down the ball and take away loft. The rule of thumb is that with the hook, you will lose two to three clubs' worth of loft . . . or put another way, a six-iron will fly like a three-iron.

To sum up:

Trust your normal swing line parallel to the body, which is aligned along the aiming point to the right, where you want the ball to start.

Do not close your stance.

Work your hands correctly so that the clubface is tilted down 45 degrees at the top of the backswing and again at the end of the stroke.

Swing normally, and let the grip, clubface alignment and ball do the rest.

21A

21B

21C

21D

22A

22B

22C

CONTROLLED SLICE

In almost every way, the slice is the direct opposite of the hook and, as any new golfer will testify, it is the easiest shot in the book. A large majority of beginners have a natural slice.

Yet, to play the ball from left to right in a deliberate, controlled way, suddenly becomes fraught with all sorts of problems.

As with the hook, the slice is a shot you will need to play in almost every round of golf if you are to save strokes, either to get around a tree or around a sharp dog-leg in the fairway.

The more you slice a shot, the more distance you will lose, yet the ball will gain height very quickly. A five-iron slice, for instance, will fly like a seven-iron and go about the same distance.

Take the standard grip, leaving the clubface square, *then* twist both hands away to the left. The ball is played from the normal position for the club you have selected (22A).

In the stance, the shoulders and feet are aligned along the aiming line. It is not an *open* stance, just a pure aim to the left towards where you want the ball to start out and then move left to right.

The takeaway (22B) is normal with the club being swung back parallel to the stance. The clubface is pointing *up* about 45 degrees and not *down* as with the hook. Again, the slicer's grip does not guarantee a slice, but it helps the necessary hand manipulation, which is aimed at getting the clubface in the correct position.

Rehearse the shot, swinging the club through slowly from waist-high to waist-high keeping the face turned up going back and coming through (22C). Programme your hands to do what you want. Visualise the effect you are seeking in the shot and soon the hands will respond to what your eyes tell them.

In actually playing the shot, there is a natural swing down and through the ball, driving along the line of aim (23A–E). Obviously, that is cutting across the direct flight to the target, but it is parallel with your body, a

23A

23B

method you have been training to use with all your golf shots. Why change now simply because there is a slice or a hook shot to be made?

I cannot emphasise this too much: **In all shots, swing parallel to your body, aiming along the line where you want the ball to start.**

After that point has been reached, the effects of arms, hands and clubface take over and direct the ball to its target, whether it be slice, hook or straight shot.

WINDY GOLF

If there is one thing many golfers worry about more than anything else it is playing on a windy day.

But, let's be realistic. Ninety-nine times out of 100 conditions are not ideal and, around Australia's coastline especially, where the main courses are located, wind is a major factor.

If you have any pretensions to playing better golf, let alone winning golf, you have to learn to not only play in the wind, but to use it as an ally.

For example, on a long par four with a following breeze, getting the ball up high to take advantage of that wind can help to cut a stroke off your usual score.

That same hole with a wind in the face can become a monster if you let it. Develop your technique for playing in wind and you will find yourself approaching that monster with confidence.

Basically, there are two ways of playing *into* the wind, perhaps the worst of situations. In both, the primary aim is to keep the ball low.

I'll come to one of the methods later. The other is the one I prefer because it works best for me. Maybe it will work for you, too, but there is only one place to find out and that is on the practice fairway.

24

The technique starts with the setup (24). The further back you set the ball and the further ahead of the clubhead you set your hands, the lower you are going to flight the ball. However, there is a cut-off point beyond which the club comes to a jarring halt. Ideally, ball placement should be no more than eight centimetres back from centre.

One of the tricks is to ensure that you do not bring your body weight back in the stance; it should be about 70 per cent on your left leg.

At the address when you look down, your head must be ahead of the ball, so too should be your hands with the left arm and clubshaft forming a straight line. Since the shot tends to produce slice, toe the clubface in slightly.

23C

23D

23E

25A

25B

Make your pivot around the left leg in the takeaway (25A) keeping the body weight forward, while the swing, as always, begins with the thrust of the knees and hips moving into the shot (25B). By the time you reach the point of impact, you have your hips opened to the target and the weight even more on the left leg (25C).

The shot itself is a punching one, taking a deepish divot. Do not let the arms quit at the vital moment but ride the clubhead down the line to the target. The follow-through (25D) will be abbreviated, but you will be well satisfied with the ball's low trajectory.

I have said before that Peter Thomson is particularly good at playing wind shots. They come out nice and low and straight, as do those of his old mate and Canada Cup partner, Kel Nagle. But then, playing on Britain's links courses, as both have done countless times, teaches one about the tricks of playing in the wind very quickly.

Instead of changing the ball position and the swing technique, Peter and Kel both like to play the ball from the normal position with a three-quarter swing using a straighter-faced club.

They will make a pitch with a five-iron to go seven-iron distance, or a

25C

25D

three-iron to travel like a five-iron in length and so on . . . and some people might prefer that method which involves a three-quarter shot to changing their technique as I do.

The easiest way to find out which is best for you is through example and observation and feel. You have already learned this three-quarter shot through practising your wedge or nine-iron.

Try it on the practice fairway by hitting a couple of true nine-iron shots for length, mark them and then take a seven. Choke it down the handle, play the ball from the normal position and hit as you would a three-quarter pitch, making the ball travel nine-iron distance with a low trajectory.

Work your way through the club-range in this way, choking the handle and playing an ordinary three-quarter shot, lengthening or shortening the swing according to the distance you want, but still accelerating through the shot.

Compare the results with the method I prefer, and adopt the one which suits you best.

Into the Wind

ROYAL MELBOURNE—
SIXTH WEST COURSE

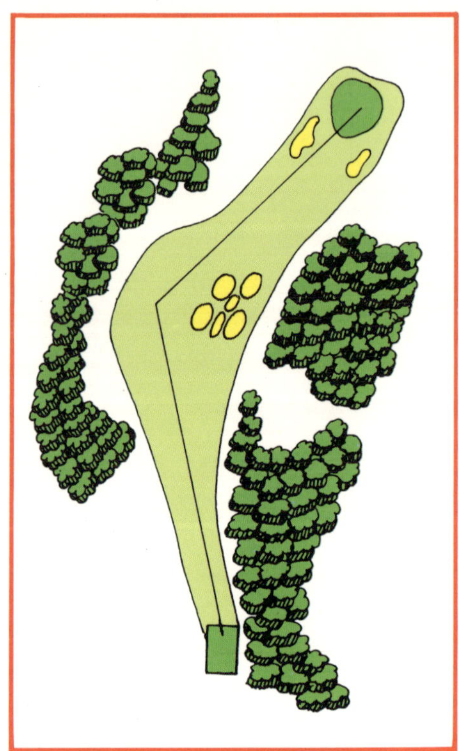

One of the simplest things I like about Royal Melbourne is the comfortable feeling of confidence one gets in playing off dry, well-cut grass with sand underneath.

A good example of this is the Sixth hole on the West Course, 391 metres dog-leg right, par four. As the ordinary golfer plays it, the Sixth is not usually a birdie chance. The way to approach playing this hole is to measure off your distances—lengths you know you can hit comfortably—and stick to them without getting ambitious.

The tee is elevated, allowing you to sum up and make your choice of clubs with most dangers in sight. Trees lining the first half of the fairway give some protection from the wind so the aim is to reach the corner away from that section's bunkers and heavy growth on the right.

Here is where it gets a little more difficult for, on reaching the corner on this day, there is a twenty-knot headwind coming down from the green.

The situation calls for a fairway wood, the intention being to lay up, as most club members do, about twenty-five metres short of the green, but keeping low with a punch shot. From here it's a pitch and run with a nine-iron to the most challenging part of this Sixth—a sloping, running green with the flag set low towards the front.

I remember Peter Thomson telling

me about the Canadian Al Balding and this Sixth during the 1959 Canada Cup, which, incidentally, was won for Australia by Peter and Kel Nagle. That day Balding overshot the green to give him a long, downhill putt. Instead of striking boldly, his attempt was more than feeble, leaving the ball a metre short and still downhill. The next attempt was too bold and the ball ran past. The next snaked on the slope past the cup, and Balding only holed out the fourth attempt through sheer desperation. The Sixth virtually destroyed him.

The green requires care and calmness, accuracy to the aiming point above the cup (in this case) and luckily, a nice, short uphill putt to hole out.

Interestingly, the records show that the average for this Sixth hole in the 1978 PGA Championship over the last two days was 4·4. Again, as with most Royal Melbourne holes, the average golfer taking a one-over is in very good company!

Danger on the Left

FIRST, THE LAKES GC, SYDNEY—
PAR FOUR, 325 METRES

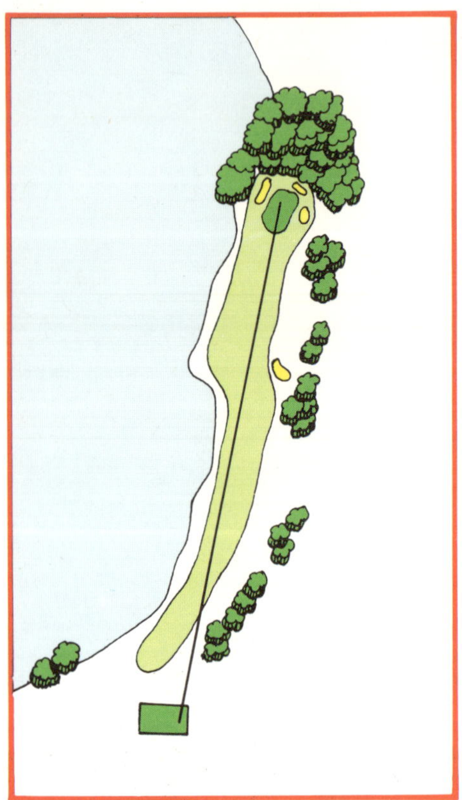

Although I have included the Lakes' First in this chapter devoted to recovery shots, very few golfers would be willing to test their skills in getting out of trouble on the left of this particular fairway.

The patch of water is more a swamp than a lake and looks very nasty. The fairway dog-legs left around this mess of trouble. Still, the good golfer will try to get near the green with his drive by cutting across the dog-leg, particularly with the breeze behind him.

If you are not feeling courageous, then aim well right with the driver—even then it is a somewhat difficult shot to judge.

From the second shot on, life on this hole is easier, usually a three-quarter nine-iron, aiming to trundle the ball up onto the green where all lines to the cup are fairly straightforward.

A Critical Hole

SEVENTH, ROYAL ADELAIDE GC—
PAR THREE, 139 METRES

I have often thought that golfers in the old days had much the better of things. The courses were rough-and-ready compared to those of today and scores were less predictable. It was bound to be more fun.

Obstacles on the course now incline to be a great deal more standard, inducing a more even standard of golf. Nevertheless, the game doesn't get any easier, and Royal Adelaide's Seventh demonstrates the need to approach every hole as a critical one.

This short par three also proves the point that a good hole doesn't need to be long to be difficult. The thick tree-line protects the first part of the tee shot but often disguises the wind direction, and the well-shaped bunkers penalise anything wayward off the tee. Normally, I would take a six-iron off the Seventh tee, but with the prevailing headwind, a five seems to be a safer choice.

The green is a good, testing one for your putting technique.

The Devil's Handiwork

ELEVENTH, THE AUSTRALIAN GC, SYDNEY—PAR THREE, 173 METRES

When the talk in the clubhouse after a tournament turns to tough, punitive holes, there is one which invariably dominates the conversation.

The Eleventh at the Australian might have been designed by the devil himself. Instead, Jack Nicklaus had a fairly big hand in it and after playing there, one might be inclined to think Jack and Nick are one and the same!

A hole that looks hard and is hard, it provides no safe side for the tee shot, no room for error. The green is long and narrow, the bunkers waiting to snap up anything but the perfect shot.

From the tee, there is only one choice—go for green-centre. The only decision to be made is with which club?—the two-iron probably, but it could be the four-wood, whichever you feel most confident will give you accuracy and length.

Now, let's say, for the sake of argument, that your tee shot missed the sand, but stopped a little short. You will find (as I have done) that the grass around the green is a little too rough for putting and calls for a chip. Then you will also find that the green is speedy and requires a careful reading.

Anyone who walks away from the Australian's Eleventh with a four on his card has every reason to smile.

A short pitch to the highly deceptive green on the Sixth Hole, West Course, Royal Melbourne.

Practice —The 10 000th Putt

Perhaps because it is a challenge to character and temperament, golf seems to attract more intensive analysis than any other sport.

To the professionals, it is a way of livelihood. To others, it is merely a way of life. As a result, all that study and analysis has produced countless theories, adages and homilies.

I must confess to having used one or two in this book, but only where they seemed appropriate to the point in hand. One I do like is Ben Hogan's: 'A golfer should never play a shot he hasn't practised recently'.

Everybody marvelled when Tom Watson holed a wedge from off the Seventeenth green at Pebble Beach for a tie-breaking birdie in the 1982 US Open. It was described as miraculous. Watson himself thought it was a pretty good shot, but nothing startling. After all, he said, he had practised the stroke thousands of times. So, too, had Ballesteros before his chip into the final hole of the 1983 US Masters.

Graham Marsh thought there was nothing extraordinary about a thirty-five-metre putt to clinch the Australian Masters at Huntingdale. It was only the 10 000th time he had struck a putt to the cup over that length.

When Hogan talked of practice, what he meant was rehearsing his shots for up to ten hours a day.

The ordinary golfer, however, is fortunate if he can get that many hours of practice in a month. His need, therefore, is to make as much use as possible of the time available for practice. But it has to be intelligent practice, not the mere slamming of a bucket full of balls. It should be aimed at overcoming the problems he has with different types of shots, and if he is at all serious about his golf, he will do this. Even ten minutes a day in the backyard can be an effective preparation for the weekend round.

Experience over the years I have been teaching has shown me that the successful pupil is the one who looks at his problems realistically and works to correct them in the amount of time he has available.

That experience has also enabled me to develop practice drills and corrective routines which have been used by many students. They may help you, too.

CORRECTIVES

Since slicing is such a natural action, the arms and wrists need training to do the unnatural. The key factor is to get the wrists twisting 45 degrees coming down into the ball and continue the movement through a further 45 degrees after impact.

The routine will be helpful in making you aware of the motion.

With the standard neutral grip, the clubface (1A) is vertical (or square to the ball at the address) as it approaches the ball. Twisting the face down (1B) will straighten the clubface for the moment of impact.

1A

1B

THE TAKEAWAY

This is one for the backyard to get you used to the correct swing action.

The upper left side turning initiates the takeaway which is not geometrically straight back off the ball as some people believe, but a gentle curve along the cartwheel line (2A).

Start down with the hips and let the body weight come through, shoulders parallel to the line, with the left arm and shaft lying along that line (2B).

2A

2B

TARGETING

Practise aiming at the target with your follow-through. Take your stance, lift the club to shoulder-height in front, turn, swing and finish with the club pointing at a pre-selected target (3A–C).

It is important to think of the swing line, rather than the stance and the final photograph shows how the club should be at the half-way point in the follow-through.

To sum up:

- Take it back on line
- Bring it down on line
- Follow through on line

3A

3B

3C

THE SHOEBOX

Another backyard routine can correct the slice or hook, or at least show you what needs to be done.

For both, the drill is easy to do and involves the use of an old shoebox or cardboard carton.

Set the box in line with your left heel, as you would a ball (4A).

Make slow-motion swings and it will seem natural to hit the box with the flat of the clubface. Mark you, the temptation to drill a hole in the box with the club will be enormous. Just swing nice and slowly, just tapping the box.

If you are a slicer, exaggerate that 45-degree twist in the downswing, (4B) and tap the box with the toe of the club.

For the hooker, keep the left hand on top for those slow-motion swings, correcting as you go (4C) and hitting the box with the heel or shaft. It needs constant training to achieve your corrective. Ten or more swings to equate to hitting one ball. So be patient and train those hands.

5

MORE ON THE SHOEBOX

The old box will come in handy, too, if you have a tendency to shank the ball.

Place the toe of the club against the box and one of those hollow plastic balls against the clubface (5).

Swing slowly, aiming to stroke the ball away without moving the box and soon you will begin to realise just where the clubhead is in the swing.

THROUGH THE GATE

Incidentally, shanking is a common fault. It is caused by one of two factors:

1. Swinging the club in a low, flat arc back behind your body.
2. The right shoulder out at the address or at the start of downswing, causing you to loop out at the top of the backswing.

A corrective and, in many ways, one of the best exercises all-round, is to set up three tee-pegs—one upright in the ground about two centimetres in front of the club toe and the other touching the heel. The third peg should be laid flat on the grass, centred between the two (6).

Swing through this gate, trying to move the centre peg away by brushing the grass.

As the peg is only a centimetre high, the exercise forces you to get right down in the stroke and, if you collect one of the outside pegs, will tell you very quickly things about

4A

4B

4C

6

your swing line and whether you are toeing or heeling.

When you become proficient at brushing away that centre peg, move the others in a little more and keep going. Tighten the gate until the tees eventually touch the club. After a spell at this exercise, you will be dead-accurate in bringing that club-head through in the right place and at the right height.

TWO CLUBS

A heavy training club can do more harm than good. A training club is usually either specifically factory-made for the purpose or an old wood with the head filled with lead.

What tends to happen is that after using one, the pupil picks up an ordinary, lighter club and then whips it away too fast in the backswing, producing faulty rhythm.

You can use two ordinary clubs, preferably irons because woods may be damaged.

Set the clubs up one on top of the other (7) and take as near to your normal grip as you can. Hold them about ten centimetres off the ground and then swing them slowly, hesitating at the top for a second before starting down. This pause is a *must* when using the heavy clubs.

Make your swing as you have been taught, left shoulder starting the take-away, knees starting the downswing with body weight moving through. And only down in the hitting zone do you whip your hands and arms through.

In this way, you will swing naturally when you return to using one club.

The exercise helps to:

- Strengthen the arm and shoulder muscles.
- Inject rhythm into the swing.
- Stop any jerking in the downswing, particularly with that hesitation at the top.
- Eventually will gain you more distance in your drives.

7

THE DOORMAT

A really good routine for the back-yard is to practise your chips and pitches off the doormat. Better to use one of those old-fashioned coir mat-ting types than to plough up the lawn with divots.

Place a shallow carton (such as a chocolate box) out on the grass about three or four paces from the mat. This will serve as a reference point since the aim of the exercise is to develop your touch for distance.

Remember that with the average chip, the balls usually lob one-third of the distance to the flag, and runs the other two-thirds. With a pitch, the ratio is reversed.

As the ball probably won't run on the back lawn like it does on the course, the intention basically is to practise the lobbing part of these shots.

First, use a seven or nine-iron for little chip shots, hitting half a dozen balls. Then, hit the same number with the wedge and sand iron. Keep widening the distance, hitting six balls with the two clubs each time.

By the time you have run out of space, usually about fifteen paces in the normal backyard, you will have begun to visualise your lobbing points for each type of stroke and so develop your touch for distance.

INDOORS PRACTICE

Any professional athlete will tell you that the biggest part of his time is not spent on the field of competition, but in practice.

It may be as high as 80 per cent for footballers. The figure for upper level golfers is probably less, given the number of tournaments they play. Where they make up the difference is in the intelligence they apply to their drills and routines and their ability to grab any moment they can to train.

On tour Lee Trevino seldom misses a chance to practise his tiny chip shots at night in his hotel room, just quietly lifting the ball a few metres into the corners of the room's couch or settee.

The ordinary golfer's game will improve if he follows the same routines as the pros, even though the

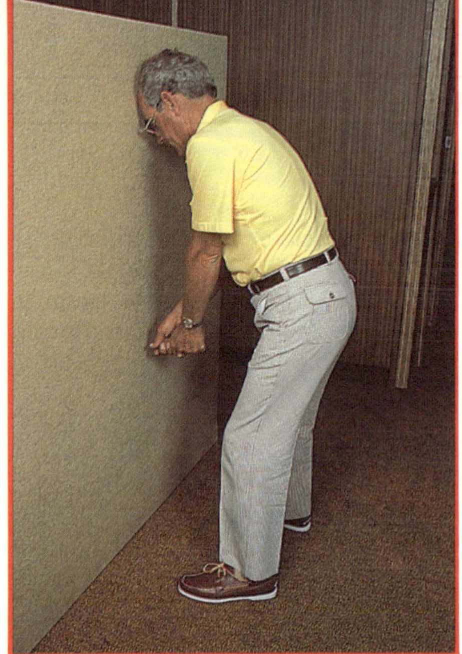
8A

8B

8C

time he has available to spend on them is far less. Your game will improve in direct proportion to the thought and effort put into practice. And you do not have to go to the golf club to do them.

We have covered some of the backyard drills already. They are aimed at curing bad habits and replacing them with the correct swing and strike patterns. Supportive routines, done indoors, can provide worthwhile results even when they may take only a few minutes of each day. A regular lunchtime session of isometric exercises, plus a few of the following drills, will do you far more good than an expense-account lunch with all the trappings.

CENTRING

If you are at all worried about centring your pivot line, here is a good way to rehearse it without the need for a club. Using a wall or door jam, maintain light pressure with your forehead as you pivot. That pressure will enable you to feel instantly any tendency to push down or pull away in the movement (8A–C).

KEEPING IN TOUCH

The other end needs attention, too!

Turn around and stand with your heels about eight or nine centimetres out from the wall, with your bottom just touching it, and pivot through your swing.

At the top of the backswing, the right hip touches the wall (9A).

In the downswing, the bottom slides along the wall (9B).

Turn through to complete the movement, ending up with the left hip against the wall (9C).

In doing this, you will learn exactly what it feels like (with a very sensitive part of the anatomy!) to pivot at an angle constant to the address.

From time to time, in television interviews, you may have heard the

9A

9B

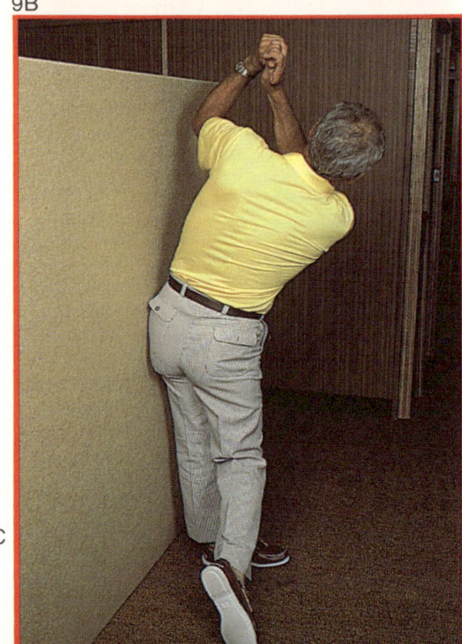
9C

pros talk about 'keeping into the shot'. This routine shows how it is done. What is more, with that wall behind you, it cannot be overdone.

PUTTING STRAIGHT

Putting is the easiest part of the game to practise indoors. Many businessmen keep an old stick in the office to do just that. But instead of aimlessly knocking balls into a cup across the room, go to the wall to practise the stroke (10).

Place the toe of the putter on the skirting board and lightly rub it back and forth, training yourself to make a straight swing.

Since you will be starting and ending on the wall, obviously you will be able to centre the ball. If yours is a wristless stroke (à la Ben Crenshaw) the putter blade will be slightly opening and closing through the swing.

If you use your wrists (as do Palmer and Casper) then observe how the blade stays 90 degrees square to the line all the way. This latter action is quite a conscious manipulation of the hands.

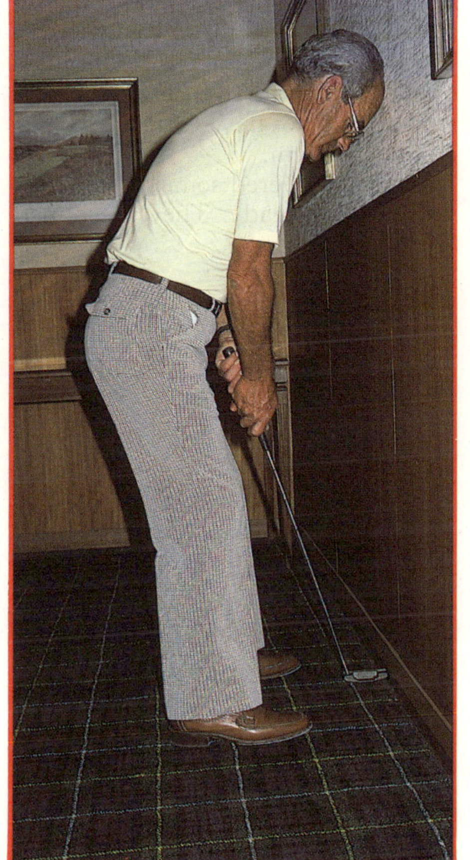

10

Whichever your style, the exercise should be done daily to maintain rhythm and line.

THE STRAIGHT LEFT

Here is another drill. Basically, it involves nothing more than pulling the straight left arm across the throat in the takeaway. Remember, it is all part of training the muscles and mind to fall into a well-rehearsed groove.

Grip the left wrist with your right hand and fold the right elbow, pointing *down.* (11A–C)

Start with the left arm in the address position, then turn back, swinging the arm *up* across the throat, and not *down* and across the chest. Complete the turn and point the left arm to the target.

The essential point is to train the left arm to swing parallel with the shoulders, hence both force-lines (shoulder turn and arm release) are travelling in the same direction on release.

11A

11B

11C

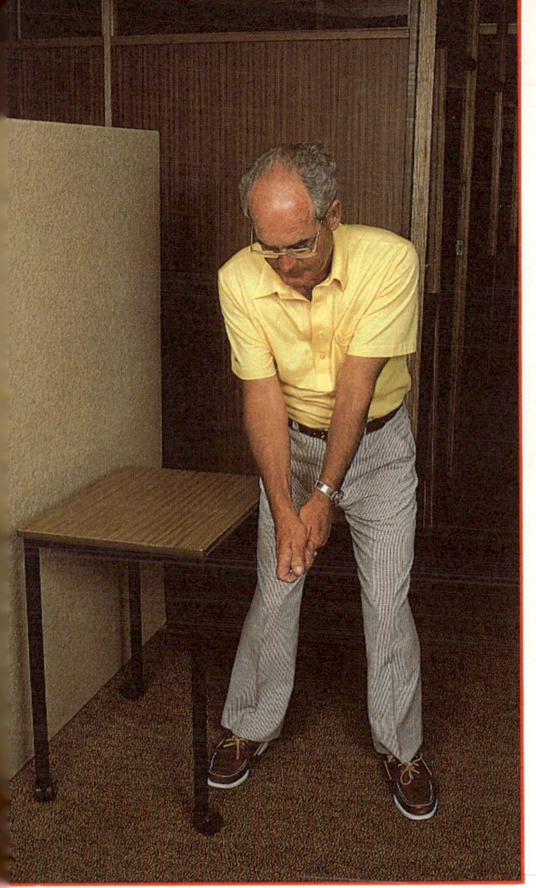
12A

12B

12C

STOP SWAYING

Finally, the problem of sway, and the solution.

Take a balanced stance with the right thigh against a desk or table (12A). Swing, letting your right hip or thigh slide back along the desk edge to a 45-degree turn. This allows the weight shift to take place correctly without a trace of sway (12B).

Now, swing through (12C) and your bottom should be about thirty centimetres away from the table edge. The exercise is ideal for people too scared to move at all in the pivot because of the likelihood of being told that they sway into the stroke.

PRESSURE

Aimless practice is a waste of time.

The pros know that if they don't adopt a thoughtful, orderly routine they will very quickly pay for the lapse. In addition, there is no substitute for practice and play. The more you play, the lower your score will be, although improvement is bound to be gradual.

I have found that one of the best ways to practise is to place yourself under pressure. It will not be to the same degree as you will find out on the course, perhaps in club competition, but it will certainly prepare you for the real thing.

A procedure I have adopted with the South Australian squad is to take them out on the practice fairway and get them to *pretend* they are on the course proper. Each imagines a certain type of fairway, one that usually gets them into trouble, and they play it several times over with the required clubs.

For most golfers, the internal build-up of pressure begins before they get anywhere near the course, especially if they are playing in a competition.

On the way to the club in the car, relax and try to visualise the shots you are going to play, in a general sense. This will prepare your mind for the round when you should be visualising each stroke before you play it. Work out your game plan and stick to it. Be patient and know your limitations.

When you reach the course, don't start cold. Before you go onto the first tee, follow that routine of swinging with the two clubs, slowly and rhythmically to stretch the muscles. During the 1982 Australian Open, Jack Nicklaus used his sand iron for loosening up. The heaviest club in the bag, he held it about thirty centimetres off the ground, simulating about the length of his driver, and then swung it gently and slowly, making full length swings, about a dozen in all.

During the round, think about what you are doing all the time. Learn to set a pattern of play by analysing each hole before and as you play it. You may not be able to approach the job of tackling a layout in the same way as a professional, but there is no reason why you shouldn't concentrate on what you are doing.

On the course, whether it's a competition or a friendly game, there is sure to be a certain amount of pressure involved, even if it is of the type you impose upon yourself. Take a couple of deep breaths every now and then.

Bobby Locke used to do that quite often, mostly just before taking a shot. Sometimes, when over a very difficult putt, he would exhale and then play the stroke with all the breath out of his body. Rifle shooters also do this just before they squeeze the trigger; it helps to steady them. Locke, by the way, always looked to be in control of himself. Although a smoker, he never smoked when playing golf. He didn't want the opposition to know if he was getting worked up or not.

ROUTINES

Another important point to keep in mind on the course is to adopt the same routine for each shot.

Recognise how many waggles and shuffles you do in your *good* shots and try to repeat them for *all* shots.

The first step in the routine is to get yourself feeling relaxed and comfortable; a deep breath and one or two practice swings can help.

Select your target. It may not necessarily be the flag or the centre of the fairway. Think about the conditions. If there is a strong wind blowing right to left, the target may have to be that big bushy tree on the right-hand side. Do not aim for aiming's sake. Think about it.

Then, having chosen the target, do not be so meticulous about taking the address that you forget about the object of the shot—to drive the clubhead and ball to the target. Remember, it is just like throwing a stone. Suddenly, the shot and probably the hole itself will become a whole lot simpler.

KEY THOUGHTS

Good golfers all have a key thought when they play. As Henry Cotton put it: 'You have to have a peg to hang your hat on'. Today's peg might be to get the left shoulder under the chin. Or, keep the pressure in the grip on the last three fingers of the left hand.

One of Jack Nicklaus' most consistent thoughts is to remind himself to complete his backswings. Cotton took it a step further by writing his thought for the day on the back of his glove. Most people I know would run out of gloves if they followed that example. But, the idea in principle generally works and most of the better golfers can retain a key thought and make it work for some time, perhaps for even a month or two until second nature returns to them. Then, they search intelligently for a new one.

None, however, goes out without a reminder about watching the ball. To some, the thought is not a conscious one, so second nature has it become for them. For me, it is a must. There has to be a focus point in every stroke, usually the back of the ball and certainly this is so in the short game. It is absolutely critical for a good round.

A FINAL THOUGHT

The strength of any golfer lies in his ability to produce shots near to the limits of his skills.

It means giving a 100 per cent effort every time he strikes the ball. At the same time, he must not be too ambitious or expect to find a magic way to become a better player overnight.

It is an attitude I find time and again when people go to their local pro in the expectation that he can provide an elixir that will work wonders on their game. They treat the pro exactly the same as they treat the local garage man. It is like driving the car into the garage, ordering four new tyres and saying, 'have it ready by four o'clock!' Many expect the same kind of service from the golf pro, wanting a new swing in one, easy lesson.

A pupil has to be patient. What you are doing in your swing is a natural thing to you. It may be incorrect, but it is natural because it is your style. The pro will show you the changes which have to be made but unless you are prepared to practise at home and on the course, you will have merely thrown your money away.

The most important part of any golf lesson is the realisation that improvement is up to you, and not the professional; he knows how to do it and wants you to know too. We have some of the best golf teachers in the world, here in Australia. It is important to them to not only help turn out the best golfers in the world, but also to help the average player to get more enjoyment out of his game.

All will help with the methods, training and practice.

If you want to play winning golf, seek their help.

The rest, then, is up to you.

The Fifth Hole on the Royal Melbourne composite course—where the bunkers on the right are veritable caverns.

Acknowledgements

The authors and publishers are grateful to the following clubs and professionals for their courtesy and help in the production of this book.

Royal Melbourne GC and Bruce Green
The Lakes GC, Sydney, and John Sheargold
Royal Adelaide GC and Alan Murray
The Grange GC, Adelaide, and John Burton
Victoria GC, Melbourne, and Brian Simpson
Metropolitan GC, Melbourne, and Brian Twite
The Australian GC, Sydney, and Daryl Welch.

Instruction Index